praise for focus on the family marriage series

This marriage study series is pure Focus on the Family—reliable, biblically sound and dedicated to reestablishing family values in today's society. This series will no doubt help a multitude of couples strengthen their relationship, not only with each other, but also with God, the *creator of marriage itself.*

Bruce Wilkinson

Author, The BreakThrough Series: *The Prayer of Jabez:*
Secrets of the Vine and *A Life God Rewards*

In this era of such need, Dr. Dobson's team has produced solid, helpful materials about Christian marriage. Even if they have been through marriage studies before, every couple—married or engaged—will benefit from this foundational study of life together. Thanks to Focus on the Family for helping set us straight in this top priority.

Charles W. Colson

Chairman, Prison Fellowship Ministries

In my 31 years as a pastor, I've officiated at hundreds of weddings. Unfortunately, many of those unions failed. I only wish the *Focus on the Family Marriage Series* had been available to me during those years. What a marvelous tool you as pastors and Christian leaders have at your disposal. I encourage you to use it to assist those you serve in building successful, healthy marriages.

H. B. London, Jr.

Vice President, Ministry Outreach/Pastoral Ministries
Focus on the Family

Looking for a prescription for a better marriage? You'll enjoy this timely and practical series!

Dr. Kevin Leman

Author, *Sheet Music: Uncovering the Secrets of*
Sexual Intimacy in Marriage

The *Focus on the Family Marriage Series* is successful because it shifts the focus from how to fix or strengthen a marriage to *who* can do it. Through this study you will learn that a blessed marriage will be the happy by-product of a closer relationship with the *creator* of marriage.

Lisa Whelchel

Author, *Creative Correction* and
The Facts of Life and Other Lessons My Father Taught Me

In a day and age where the covenant of marriage is so quickly tossed aside in the name of incompatibility and irreconcilable differences, a marriage Bible study that is both inspirational and practical is desperately needed. The *Focus on the Family Marriage Series* is what couples are seeking. I give my highest recommendation to this Bible study series that has the potential to dramatically impact and improve marriages today. Marriage is not so much about finding the right partner as it is about being the right partner. These studies give wonderful biblical teachings for helping those who want to learn the beautiful art of being and becoming all that God intends in their marriage.

Lysa TerKeurst

President, Proverbs 31 Ministries
Author, *Capture His Heart* and *Capture Her Heart*

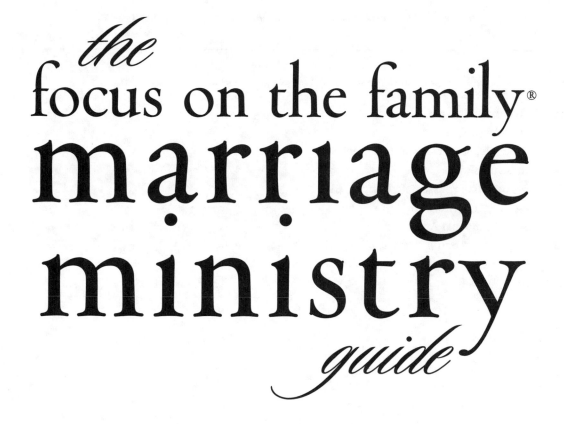

the
focus on the family®
marriage
ministry
guide

Gospel Light

Gospel Light is an evangelical Christian publisher dedicated to serving the local church. We believe God's vision for Gospel Light is to provide church leaders with biblical, user-friendly materials that will help them evangelize, disciple and minister to children, youth and families.

It is our prayer that this Gospel Light resource will help you discover biblical truth for your own life and help you minister to others. May God richly bless you.

For a free catalog of resources from Gospel Light, please call your Christian supplier or contact us at 1-800-4-GOSPEL *or* www.gospellight.com

PUBLISHING STAFF

William T. Greig, Chairman

Kyle Duncan, Publisher

Dr. Elmer L. Towns, Senior Consulting Publisher

Pam Weston, Senior Editor

Patti Pennington Virtue, Associate Editor

Hilary Young, Editorial Assistant

Jessie Minassian, Editorial Assistant

Bayard Taylor, M.Div., Senior Editor, Biblical and Theological Issues

Samantha A. Hsu, Cover and Internal Designer

Marcia L. Gillis, Writer/Compiler

ISBN 0-8307-3235-7
© 2003 Focus on the Family
All rights reserved.
Printed in the U.S.A.

How to Make Clean Copies from This Book

You may make copies of portions of this book with a clean conscience if
- you (or someone in your organization) are the original purchaser;
- you are using the copies you make for a noncommercial purpose (such as teaching or promoting your ministry) within your church or organization;
- you follow the instructions provided in this book.

However, it is illegal for you to make copies if
- you are using the material to promote, advertise or sell a product or service other than for your ministry fund-raising;
- you are using the material in or on a product for sale; or
- you or your organization are not the original purchaser of this book.

By following these guidelines you help us keep our products affordable.

Thank you,
Gospel Light

table of contents

foreword

The most urgent mission field on Earth is not across the sea or even across the street—it's right where you live: in your home and family. Jesus' last instruction was to "make disciples of all nations" (Matthew 28:19). At the thought of this command, our eyes look across the world for our work field. That's not bad; it's just not *all*. God intended the home to be the first place of Christian discipleship and growth (see Deuteronomy 6:4-8). Our family members must be the *first* ones we reach out to in word and example with the gospel of the Lord Jesus Christ, and the fundamental way in which this occurs is through the marriage relationship.

Divorce, blended families, the breakdown of communication and the complexities of daily life are taking a devastating toll on the God-ordained institutions of marriage and family. We do not need to look hard or search far for evidence that even Christian marriages and families are also in a desperate state. In response to the need to build strong Christ-centered marriages and families, this series was developed.

Focus on the Family is well known and respected worldwide for its steadfast dedication to preserving the sanctity of marriage and family life. I can think of no better partnership than the one formed by Focus on the Family and Gospel Light to produce the *Focus on the Family Marriage Series*. This series is well-written, biblically sound and right on target for guiding couples to explore the foundation God has laid for marriage and to see Him as the role model for the perfect spouse. Through this series, seeds will be planted that will germinate in your heart and mind for many years to come.

In our practical, bottom-line culture, we often want to jump over the *why* and get straight to the *what*. We think that by *doing* the six steps or *learning* the five ways, we will reach the goal. But deep-rooted growth is slower and more purposeful and begins with a well-grounded understanding of God's divine design. Knowing why marriage exists is crucial to making the how-tos more effective. Marriage is a gift from God, a unique and distinct covenant relationship through which His glory and goodness can resonate, and it is only through knowing the architect and His plan that we will build our marriage on the surest foundation.

God created marriage; He has a specific purpose for it, and He is committed to filling with fresh life and renewed strength each union yielded to Him. God wants to gather the hearts of every couple together, unite them in love and walk them to the finish line—all in His great grace and goodness.

May God, in His grace, lead you into His truth and strengthen you as you minister to the marriages in your church.

Gary T. Smalley
Founder and Chairman of the Board
Smalley Relationship Center

introduction

At the beginning of creation God "made them male and female." "For this reason a man will leave his father and mother and be united to his wife, and the two will become one flesh." So they are no longer two, but one.
Mark 10:6-8

According to nationwide studies, each year over 1 million children in the United States will suffer through the divorce of their parents. In fact, these studies show that 50 percent of the children born to married parents this year will see their parents divorce before they reach the age of 18—and the physical, emotional and financial effects of divorce will linger on these children well into their adulthood, affecting future generations as well. "Restoring the importance of marriage to society and the welfare of children will require politicians and civic and church leaders to make this one of their most important tasks."[1]

Unfortunately, Christian marriages suffer the same statistical failures as non-Christian marriages. This happens in spite of a wealth of available marriage-strengthening resources. Why? Perhaps it's time for some evaluation. It may be time to stop the flurry of church activity and think about both our ministry successes and our failures. "Perhaps"? and "may be"? Somehow those words don't seem strong enough. We live in desperate times and *now* is the time to take some serious steps to restore the sanctity of marriage.

Building a marriage ministry may seem like a daunting task; however, we encourage you to rely on the Lord for strength and wisdom as you seek to bring the sanctity of marriage back into your community and church!

The *Focus on the Family Marriage Series* is based on Al Janssen's *The Marriage Masterpiece*, an insightful look at what marriage can—and should—be.[2] Leaders of the Bible studies are encouraged to read the book for a better understanding of the concepts being presented in the series.

About the *Focus on the Family Marriage Series*

The *Focus on the Family Marriage Series* Bible studies can be used in a variety of situations, including small-group Bible studies, Sunday School classes or counseling or mentoring situations. An individual couple can also use them as an at-home marriage-building study.

Each Bible study consists of four sessions, which contain four main components.

Session Overview

Tilling the Ground

This is an introduction to the topic being discussed—commentary and questions to direct your thoughts toward the main idea of the session.

Planting the Seed

This is the Bible study portion in which Scripture is read and questions answered to help discover lasting truths from God's Word.

Watering the Hope

This is a time for discussion. Whether you are using the study at home as a couple, in a small group or in a classroom setting, talking about the lesson with others is a great way to solidify the truth and plant it deeply into your hearts.

Harvesting the Fruit

As a point of action, this portion of the session offers suggestions on putting the truth of the Word into action in the marriage relationship.

Suggestions for Group Study

There are many ways that the studies can be used in a group situation. The most common would be in a small-group Bible study format. However, they can also be used in adult Sunday School classes, weekend retreats and marriage preparation classes. However you choose to use them, there are some general guidelines to follow for group study.

- Keep the group small—five to six couples is probably the maximum.
- Ask couples to commit to regular attendance for the four weeks of the study. Regular attendance is a key to building relationships and trust in a group.
- Encourage participants *not* to share anything of a personal or potentially embarrassing nature without first asking the spouse's permission.
- Whatever is discussed in the group meetings is to be held in strictest confidence among group members only.

There are additional leader helps in the back of each Bible study. The information in this marriage ministry guide will give additional aid in guiding group studies that will build and strengthen marriages in your church and community.

Suggestions for Mentoring or Counseling Relationships

The studies also lend themselves for use in relationships where one couple mentors or counsels another couple. See chapter 6 for more information on mentoring.

- A mentoring relationship, where a couple that has been married for several years is assigned to meet on a regular basis with a younger couple, could be arranged through a system set up by a church or ministry.
- A less formal way to start a mentoring relationship is for a younger couple to take the initiative and approach a couple that exemplifies a mature, godly marriage and ask them to meet with them on a regular basis. Or the reverse might be a mature couple that approaches a younger couple to begin a mentoring relationship.
- When asked to mentor, some might shy away and think that they could never do that, knowing that their own marriage is less than perfect. But just as we are to disciple new believers, we must learn to disciple married couples to strengthen marriages in this difficult world. The Lord has promised to be "with you always" (Matthew 28:20).
- Before you begin to mentor a couple, first complete the study yourselves. This will serve to strengthen your own marriage and prepare you for leading another couple.
- Be prepared to learn as much or more than the couple(s) you will mentor.

Suggestions for Individual Couple Study

There are at least three options for using each study as a couple.

- It may be used as a devotional study that each spouse would study individually through the week; then on a specified day, the couple comes together and discusses what they have learned and how to apply it to their marriage.
- The couple might choose to study one session together in an evening and then work on the application activities during the rest of the week.
- Because of the short length of this study, it is a great resource for a weekend retreat. A couple could take a trip away for the weekend and study each session together, interspersed with favorite leisure activities.

Guidelines for Leading the Bible Studies

1. If at all possible, the group should be led by a married couple. This does not mean that both spouses need to be leading the discussions; perhaps one spouse is better at facilitating discussions while the other is better at relationship building or organization—but the leader couple should share responsibilities wherever possible.

2. At the first meeting, be sure to lay down the ground rules for discussions, stressing that following these rules will help everyone feel comfortable during discussion times.
   a. No one should share anything of a personal or potentially embarrassing nature without first asking his or her spouse's permission.
   b. Whatever is discussed in the group meetings is to be held in strictest confidence among group members only.
   c. Allow everyone in the group to participate. However, as a leader, don't force anyone to answer a question if he or she is reluctant. Be sensitive to the different personalities and communication styles among your group members.

3. Fellowship time is very important in building small-group relationships. Providing beverages and/or light refreshments either before or after each session will encourage a time of informal fellowship.

4. Most people live very busy lives; respect the time of your group members by beginning and ending meetings on time.

How to Use the Bible Studies

1. Each session of the *Focus on the Family Marriage Series* Bible studies has more than enough material to cover in a 45-minute teaching period. You will probably not have time to discuss every single question in each session, so prepare for each meeting by selecting questions you feel are most important to address for your group; discuss other questions as time permits. Be sure to save the last 10 minutes of your meeting time for each couple to interact individually and to pray together before adjourning.

> ***Optional Eight-Session Plan***—*You can easily divide each session into two parts if you'd like to cover all of the material presented in each session. Each section of the session has enough questions to divide in half, and the Bible-study sections (Planting the Seed) are divided into two or three sections that can be taught in separate sessions.*

2. Each spouse should have his or her own copy of the book in order to personally answer the questions. The general plan of each study is that the couples complete the questions at home during the week and then bring their books to the meeting to share what they have learned during the week.

   However, the reality of leading small groups in this day and age is that some members will find it difficult to do the homework. If you find that to be the case with your group, consider adjusting the lessons and having members complete the study during your meeting time as you guide them through the lesson. If you use this method, be sure to encourage members to share their individual answers with their spouses during the week (perhaps on a date night).

Notes

1. Patrick F. Fagan and Robert E. Rector, "The Effects of Divorce on America," The Heritage Foundation. http://www.heritage.org/Research/Family/BG1373.cfm (accessed January 2003).
2. Al Janssen, *The Marriage Masterpiece* (Wheaton, IL: Tyndale House Publishers, 2001).

getting started

The next day Moses took his seat to serve as judge for the people, and they stood around him from morning till evening. When his father-in-law saw all that Moses was doing for the people, he said, "What is this you are doing for the people? Why do you alone sit as judge, while all these people stand around you from morning till evening?…What you are doing is not good. You and these people who come to you will only wear yourselves out. The work is too heavy for you; you cannot handle it alone. But select capable men from all the people —men who fear God, trustworthy men who hate dishonest gain."
Exodus 18:13-21

It's no secret: Many marriages are not the masterpieces God intended them to be. Also, the Church, for the most part, is not functioning as it should in providing strong foundations for marriages and families to flourish. It's not hard to see how these two facts are connected and that the Church, when functioning as it should, can help couples remain faithful to their vows. Those whose passion is to restore marriages all face the same challenge: where to begin.

The first and most important partner we can have—in any endeavor—is God, our creator and our Lord. The task of developing a marriage ministry is huge, and you will need God's strength and guidance every step of the way as you work to develop a successful ministry.

Second, you need to partner with others who are like-minded—those in your church and community who feel a burden to strengthen marriages. Bring together godly people who are blessed with solid marriages. As you meet with them, discuss the divorce rate and the urgency of the task at hand. Pray together for God's guidance. Ask them to ; riage ministry. *The Focus on the Family Marriage Ministry Guide* will guide you in the task.

Plans fail for lack of counsel, but with many advisers they succeed.
Proverbs 15:22

SEEKING GOD'S GUIDANCE THROUGH FOCUSED PRAYER

If my people, who are called by my name, will humble themselves and pray and seek my face and turn from their wicked ways, then will I hear from heaven and will forgive their sin and will heal their land.
2 Chronicles 7:14

You guide me with your counsel.
Psalm 73:24

Consider the following true story:

It was 1872 and the evangelist Dwight L. Moody was in London and had agreed to speak at a church prayer meeting. "I preached with no unusual power," he recalled. "In fact, I was a little disappointed. I didn't seem to have much liberty there."

That evening he returned to the same church and preached again. This time, though, the results were quite different. "There seemed to be great power, as if the building was filled with the glory of God, and I asked for an expression of faith when I finished. People rose by the hundreds." Same preacher—different results—why?

For months Moody asked the same question, puzzling over the contrast. Then it became plain when he discovered that around noon that Sunday, a bedridden woman heard about his visit to the church. She had interceded and fasted for Moody and the congregants throughout the afternoon and evening. "And that night while I was preaching, she was praying, and in answer to her prayer the power of God fell upon the audience," explained Moody. "I believe when God's books are opened, there will be some hidden people who will be much nearer to the throne than you or I."

Moody's experience is repeated throughout history. Prayer is always behind a great move of God! If you look behind the scenes of a ministry that has had significant spiritual impact, you will find an individual or small group of people who have sacrificed many hours in prayer.[1]

Prayer—Divine Communication

Prayer gives eyes to our faith. In prayer we see beyond our own inadequacies and focus our spiritual eyes on the infinite power of our heavenly Father. In prayer we surrender our problems to God and indicate our trust in Him by asking for divine intervention. In Psalm 145:18 David wrote, "The LORD is near to all who call on him, to all who call on him in truth."

Prayer is not optional for the daily life of a Christian, and it is not optional for ministry to accomplish its goals! Certainly we should not attempt to develop and carry out a successful marriage ministry—or any ministry, for that matter—without continual prayer. Satan is out to destroy marriages, and he would like to see any ministry designed to strengthen marriages fail. Fortunately, we have been given specific weapons to fight against the devil, as Paul pointed out in Ephesians 6:10-18:

Finally, be strong in the Lord and in his mighty power. Put on the full armor of God so that you can take your stand against the devil's schemes. For our struggle is not against flesh and blood, but against the rulers, against the authorities, against the powers of this dark world and against the spiritual forces of evil in the heavenly realms. Therefore put on the full armor of God, so that when the day of evil comes, you may be able to stand your ground, and after you have done everything, to stand. Stand firm then, with the belt of truth buckled around your waist, with the breastplate of righteousness in place, and with your feet fitted with the readiness that comes from the gospel of peace. In addition to all this, take up the shield of faith, with which you can extinguish all the flaming arrows of the evil one. Take the helmet of salvation and the sword of the Spirit, which is the word of God. And pray in the Spirit on all occasions with all kinds of prayers and requests. With this in mind, be alert and always keep on praying for all the saints.

Through prayer, we align ourselves with God's purposes and open ourselves to receive His guidance. Proverbs 19:21 says, "Many are the plans in a man's heart, but it is the LORD's purpose that prevails." Paul explained in Romans 8:26-28 that the Holy Spirit will help us as we pray:

In the same way, the Spirit helps us in our weakness. We do not know what we ought to pray for, but the Spirit himself intercedes for us with groans that words cannot express. And he who searches our hearts knows the mind of the Spirit, because the Spirit intercedes for the saints in accordance with God's will. And we know that in all things God works for the good of those who love him, who have been called according to his purpose.

Why Do We Pray?

According to Judith Couchman, there are eight reasons to pray for your ministry.

1. Jesus calls us to pray persistently (see Luke 18:1-7).
2. The devil will devour whomever and whatever he can (see 1 Peter 5:7-9).
3. We gain wisdom and guidance (see James 1:5).
4. Every ministry requires resources (see Philippians 4:6-7).
5. Prayer ignites spiritual power (see Ephesians 3:16-19).
6. Prayer triggers fruitfulness (see Colossians 1:9-12).
7. Everyone faces temptation (see Matthew 26:41).
8. Sometimes we need a miracle (Mark 11:23-24).[2]

Where and When Should We Pray?

Prayer is needed in every aspect of our lives, from our everyday lives to our planning for leadership meetings. In Scripture we are told:

- "Pray continually" (1 Thessalonians 5:17).
- "In everything, by prayer and petition, with thanksgiving, present your requests to God" (Philippians 4:6).
- "Pray in the Spirit on all occasions with all kinds of prayers and requests. With this in mind, be alert and always keep on praying for all the saints" (Ephesians 6:18).
- "Glory in his holy name; let the hearts of those who seek the LORD rejoice. Look to the LORD and his strength; seek his face always" (Psalm 105:3-4).

How Do We Pray?

The Lord's Prayer (see Matthew 6:9-13) serves as a basic model for us. There are also many other passages that can help us move our leaders, couples and groups to a deeper relationship with God through prayer. Colossians 1 provides us with a pattern we can follow when we pray for others (for a reproducible copy of this prayer pattern, see p. 20).

Personalizing and praying an actual Scripture passage is a very powerful way to pray. The following pages give you examples of personalized passages. Additional materials have been provided that will also help you, your leaders and the couples to whom you are ministering be more effective in prayer. Discuss them and use them together with your leaders and couples in your group.

In your evaluation and planning meetings, pray specifically that the Lord will guide and direct you in your time together.

Notes
1. Judith Couchman, "Is Part of Your Team Missing?" *Discipleship Journal*, vol. 22, no. 6 (November/December 2002), pp. 82-83.
2. Ibid.

The Patterns of Prayer

This is a scriptural guide to the pattern of prayer.

Opening   Hear our prayer (see Nehemiah 1:11; Psalm 5:1-3).

Adoration   Holy is your name (see Deuteronomy 10:21; 1 Chronicles 29:10-13; Psalm 34:8-9).

Affirmation   Your will be done (see Psalm 27:1; Isaiah 26:3, Romans 8:38-39).

Requests   Give us this day (see Psalm 7:1; Nehemiah 1:11; Matthew 7:7-8).

Confession   Forgive us (see Psalm 51; 1 John 1:9; Matthew 18:21-22).

Renewal   "Lead us not into temptation" (Matthew 6:13; Luke 11:4).

Blessing   "The Lord bless you and keep you" (Numbers 6:24).

What to Pray for Others

These verses will guide you in your prayers for others.

For this reason, since the day we heard about you, we have not stopped praying for you and asking God to fill you with the knowledge of his will through all spiritual wisdom and understanding. And we pray this in order that you may live a life worthy of the Lord and may please him in every way: bearing fruit in every good work, growing in the knowledge of God, being strengthened with all power according to his glorious might so that you may have great endurance and patience, and joyfully giving thanks to the Father, who has qualified you to share in the inheritance of the saints in the kingdom of light. For he has rescued us from the dominion of darkness and brought us into the kingdom of the Son he loves, in whom we have redemption, the forgiveness of sins (Colossians 1:9-14).

Colossians 1:9
- Spiritual wisdom and an understanding of God's will

Colossians 1:10
- A life that is pleasing to the Lord in every way
- Bountiful harvests from good works

Colossians 1:11
- Strength, endurance and patience through reliance on God

Colossians 1:12
- A thankful heart for God's amazing love

Colossians 1:13-14
- Acknowledgment of Christ's sacrifice
- Acceptance of the forgiveness offered for our sins through Christ

Praying Scripture Prayers

The following verses are examples of how to pray by personalizing Scripture:

O Lord, I have no desire to listen to those whose advice is not reflecting Your heart. Bless me as one who does not listen to those who speak against You. I delight in Your Word, Lord, and find comfort in it day and night. Father, bless me that my life might yield fruit for Your kingdom. Help me, God, to seek You in all I do so that I may prosper in Your will (see Psalm 1:1-3).

I praise You, Lord, for Your wisdom and Your counsel, which never ceases. Thank You, Father, for always speaking to my heart, day and night. I praise Your holy name and know that because You are with me at all times, I cannot be shaken (see Psalm 16:7-8).

Father, it is You who turns darkness to light. It is You who is perfect in all You do and all You say. It is You who is my shield, my refuge and my rock. It is You who is the Alpha and Omega, Lord, the beginning and the end. There is no other Lord but You (see Psalm 18:28-31; Revelation 1:8).

O Lord, You said "The greatest among you will be your servant. For whoever exalts himself will be humbled, and whoever humbles himself will be exalted" (Matthew 23:11-12). Help me, Jesus, to walk humbly before You and to be Your servant.

Dear God, make my attitude the same as that of Christ, "who, being in very nature God, did not consider equality with God something to be grasped, but made himself nothing, taking the very nature of a servant, being made in human likeness. And being found in appearance as a man, he humbled himself and became obedient to death—even death on a cross" (Philippians 2:6-8).

Scripture Prayers for Couples

For Wives

Lord, help me to be a woman worthy of respect. Help me, Father, to be kind in words and deeds and to be trustworthy in all You have entrusted to me (see 1 Timothy 3:11).

(Other Scriptures to pray: Ephesians 5:21-24,33; 1 Peter 3:1-6.)

For Husbands

Lord, help me to be a considerate husband. Help me to remember that my wife is an heir to Your gracious gift of life. May my actions be transparent before You (see 1 Peter 3:7).

(Other Scriptures to pray: Ephesians 5:21,25-33.)

For Husbands and Wives Together

Lord, thank You for our marriage. Help us to honor one another even above ourselves, remaining humble and respectful of one another in all circumstances. Help us to stay pure and faithful in all aspects of our marriage, being content with what You have given us in all areas of our life together; and help us, Lord, to forgive each other with the same compassion and kindness that Christ has shown toward us (see Romans 12:10-11; Hebrews 13:4-5; Ephesians 4:32).

STUDYING KEY ISSUES

After you have assembled a core group of individuals who want to help strengthen the marriages in your church and community, the next step to building your marriage ministry is to discover together the answers to the following questions (this will likely take several meetings):

- What specific things does the Bible say about marriage?
- What are the current trends, mind-sets and philosophies that affect the longevity of today's marriages?
- What is the primary source of the breakdown of marriages?
- What is our church currently doing to strengthen marriages?
- What more can we do to strengthen marriages in our church *and* community?
- What are other churches in our area doing to strengthen marriages and how can we join forces with them?
- What, if any, are the local community support groups that we can join forces with and learn from?

The following reproducible pages will help your group discover the answers to these important questions. There is also a survey that should be given to engaged couples, newlyweds and couples that have been married several years.

Note: *It is strongly suggested that the couples who are involved in developing a ministry to marriages complete* The Masterpiece Marriage, *the foundational study in the* Focus on the Family Marriage Series. *You are also encouraged to read* The Marriage Masterpiece *(by Al Janssen), the book on which the whole series of studies is based.*

What Does the Bible Say About Marriage?

Read Genesis 2:21-24; Matthew 19:4-8 and Ephesians 5:21-33.

1. How does the fact that God chose to create Eve out of Adam's own rib point to God's purpose for marriage?

2. What do these verses reveal about the nature of the marriage relationship?

3. How do these verses indicate that God intended for a marital relationship to be permanent?

4. What do these verses tell you about God's purpose for marriage?

Reproducible

God's Plan for Marriage

Write your thoughts about marriage as God intended it to be.

Its Purpose

Its Nature

God's Plan for Marriage

Write your thoughts about marriage as God intended it to be.

Its Purpose

Its Nature

Marriage as a Covenant Relationship

The word "covenant" is used nearly 300 times in the Bible. The first mention occurs in Genesis 6:18 when God established a covenant with Noah (see also Genesis 9:8-17; 17:9-14). God then entered into a covenant with Abraham (see Genesis 15:1-8) and the children of Israel (see Exodus 24:1-11; 34:27-28). In Jeremiah 31, God refers to a "new covenant" (v. 31) that He will make with His people in which He "will put my law in their minds and write it on their hearts" (v. 33). This refers to the new covenant of grace that we have through Jesus Christ (see Galatians 3:26-29).

Study the concept of covenant throughout the Bible—a foundational concept to understanding God's plan. As you study, consider the following questions:

- What characterized the covenants that God made with mankind?
- What characterizes the covenants that humans make with one another?

1. According to 1 Samuel 18:1-5, what three things accompanied the covenant between Jonathan and David?

2. What did Jonathan do as a sign of his covenant with David?

"In covenant, two become one. When you and I repent and receive the Lord Jesus Christ, we enter into the New Covenant of Grace, merging ourselves in Him. We in Him and He in us. In doing so we, in essence, put on His robe. We are to become like Christ."[1]

Read Genesis 2:21-24; Matthew 19:4-8 and Ephesians 5:31-33 before answering the following questions:

3. What indication do we have that marriage is a covenant relationship?

4. As a covenant relationship, marriage should have what as its characteristics?

 **Note:** *For further study of the covenant relationship in marriage, go through* The Covenant Marriage— *one of the* Focus on the Family Marriage Series *studies—together.*

Note

1. *Covenant Student Guide* (Chattanooga, TN: Precept Ministries International, 1994), p. 7.

Current Trends

Americans and Theology

Make note of the staggering misconceptions held by a large portion of the American public.

- 59 percent reject the existence of Satan.
- 50 percent argue that a person can earn a place in heaven by doing good rather than by a relationship with Jesus Christ and God's grace.
- 44 percent contend that the Bible, the Koran and the Book of Mormon are all different expressions of the same spiritual truths.
- 54 percent believe that truth can be discovered only through logic, human reasoning and personal experience.[1]
- 72 percent think that people are blessed by God, so they can enjoy life as much as possible.[2]

Americans and Truth

More and more Americans are buying into the concept that truth is dependent on an individual's own interpretation of truth. The frightening news is that even Christians are buying into the concept that truth is relative!

- 64 percent of adults and 83 percent of teenagers believe that truth is always relative to the person involved and the situation or circumstances.
- 6 percent of teenagers said moral truth is absolute.
- 32 percent of Christian adults believe in moral absolutes, compared to just half as many (15 percent) among non-Christians. Only 9 percent of Christian teens indicated a belief in moral absolutes compared to 4 percent of non-Christian teens.
- 31 percent of adults and 38 percent of teens indicated that their most common basis for moral decision making is doing whatever feels right or comfortable in a situation.
- 15 percent of adults make moral decisions based upon values they learned from their parents; 13 percent base their decisions on biblical principles and 10 percent base their decisions on whatever outcome will produce the most personally beneficial results.
- 7 percent of teens make moral decisions based upon biblical principles; 16 percent base their decisions on whatever would produce the most personally beneficial results.
- Adults age 36 or older are more than twice as likely as 18- to 35-year-olds to base moral choices on biblical principles (18 percent versus 7 percent).
- 52 percent of young adults and 54 percent of teenagers base their moral choices on feelings and beneficial outcomes compared to just 32 percent of adults 36 and older who do so.[3]

Americans and Marriage

- More than 80 percent of married adults say they have a happy marriage.
- 75 percent of married adults would marry the same person again.
- 80 percent of adults who have never been married say they would like to get married.[4]
- 33 percent of all born-again individuals who have been married have gone through a divorce (statistically identical to the 34 percent incidence among non-born-again adults).
- 33 percent of adults have cohabited with a nonfamily member of the opposite sex.
- In the year 2000 there were 2.4 million grandparents who acted as the primary caregivers for their grandchildren, as a result of divorce and other factors.[5]
- 56 percent of American adults are married.[6]
- 44 percent of American adults under 35 have cohabited, compared to 33 percent of those aged 35 to 49, 24 percent of those aged 50 to 69 and 1 percent of those in their 70s.
- 25 percent of Christians have cohabited as compared to 37 percent of those who call themselves Christians but do not have Christian belief systems.[7]

American Adults and Church Attendance

- 68 percent of adults 55 and older who attended church regularly as children still attend.
- 53 percent of adults under 35 who attended church regularly as children still attend.
- More than 30 percent of adults 35 and older who did not attend a Christian church as a child do so now, compared to 16 percent of those younger than 35.
- People who attended church as children are twice as likely to read their Bible and attend a church worship service each week, and are nearly 50 percent more likely to pray to God during the week.[8]

And finally (and sadly), a challenge to churches from findings by the Marriage Covenant Movement:

- The majority of people making a first-time decision for Christ are no longer connected to a Christian church within eight weeks of their decision.[9]

Notes

1. "Americans Draw Theological Beliefs from Diverse Points of View," *Barna Research Group, Ltd.*, October 8, 2002. http://www.barna.org/cgi-bin/PagePressRelease.asp?PressReleaseID=122&Reference=B.
2. George Barna, *The Second Coming of the Church* (Nashville, TN: Word Publishing, 1998), p. 21.
3. "Americans Are Most Likely to Base Truth on Feelings," *Barna Research Group, Ltd.*, February 12, 2002. http://www.barna.org/cgi-bin/PagePressRelease.asp?PressReleaseID=106&Reference=B.
4. George Barna and Mark Hatch, *Boiling Point: It Only Takes One Degree* (Ventura, CA: Regal Books, 2001), p. 42.
5. U.S. Census Bureau, "Grandparents as Caregivers," *Profile of Selected Social Characteristics: 2000*, Census 2000, Table DP-2. http://www.censtats.census.gov/data/US/01000.pdf (accessed October 2002).
6. Glenn T. Stanton, *Why Marriage Matters: Reasons to Believe in Marriage in Postmodern Society* (Colorado Springs, CO: Pinon Press, 1997), pp. 58-59.
7. "Born Again Adults Less Likely to Co-Habit, Just as Likely to Divorce," *Barna Research Group, Ltd.*, August 6, 2001. http://www.barna.org/cgibin/PagePressRelease.asp?PressReleaseID=95&Reference=B.
8. "Adults Who Attended Church as Children Show Lifetime Effects," *Barna Research Group, Ltd.*, November 5, 2001. http://www.barna.org/cgi-bin/PagePressRelease.asp?PressReleaseID=101&Reference=B.
9. Barna, *The Second Coming of the Church*, p. 2.

Marriage Ministry Survey

Name (Optional) _____

Age Group

     ___ 18 to 25   ___ 45 to 55

     ___ 25 to 35   ___ 55+

     ___ 35 to 45

1. How long have you been a Christian?

2. How long have you been a growing Christian?

3. How long have you been attending church in general?

4. How long have you been attending this church?

5. How often do you attend Sunday School?

     ___ Regularly

     ___ Sporadically

     ___ Other (Please explain.)

6. How often do you attend a home group or other small-group Bible study?

     ___ Regularly

     ___ Sporadically

     ___ Other (Please explain.)

7. What, if any, other types of discipleship opportunities have you been involved in?

     ___ Conferences   ___ Mentoring relationships

     ___ Counseling   ___ Retreats

     ___ Elective classes   ___ Support groups

     ___ Other (Please explain.)

8. Do you feel that our church provides adequate help for people who are considering marriage? If yes, please explain.

If no, what helps would you like to see implemented?

9. If you have attended marriage (or premarriage) classes or groups, what was done to make it more likely that you would apply the marriage principles taught?

10. In what ways has our church helped you in your marriage (or premarriage) relationship?

11. What are some ways our church could better help you or others develop a stronger marriage relationship?

Marriage Ministry Survey Evaluation Sheet

Summarize the surveys using the following questions:

1. What is our church doing to strengthen marriages?

2. How effective has each aspect of our church's marriage ministry been?

3. What suggestions were given by those surveyed?

Staff Survey

In order to best serve our couples in this marriage ministry, please take a few moments to answer each of the following questions to the best of your knowledge:

1. Do we have a written church policy that establishes our marriage philosophies, goals and programs?

2. Does this policy list any requirements that must be fulfilled before we allow a couple to marry at our church (e.g., premarital counseling)? If so, what are they?

3. Does this policy address such issues as marrying divorcees, a couple that are cohabiting, a believer marrying a nonbeliever, a nonbeliever marrying another nonbeliever, etc.? What does it say?

4. Do we offer any type of discipleship, premarital, marriage enrichment or other marriage development programs on a regular basis? If so, what do we offer?

5. What types of resources do we use? List books, study guides and other materials.

6. Do we team up with other churches or other community or nationwide marriage organizations? If so, which ones?

7. Which staff members are assigned to provide premarital preparation, perform marriages and oversee marital development in our church?

8. What is included in the premarital preparation we offer? (For example: Does it include a premarital personality exam, specific topics, a certain number of sessions, a premarriage mentoring agreement with an older marriage-seasoned couple, etc.?)

building a marriage ministry

As you prepare to build your marriage ministry, don't allow yourself to feel personally responsible for creating every aspect of a comprehensive program. A lot of practical information and resources are included in this guide to help you in the development process. You may also be able to borrow ideas from other quality marriage ministries in your community. Network with other churches, utilizing marriage-strengthening ministries they have already developed to also strengthen the marriages in your church, and invite them to make use of other ministries you might already have in place.

Characteristics of a Successful Ministry

We know that you want to build a marriage ministry that is successful. How can you recognize a successful marriage ministry? Such a ministry exhibits the following characteristics:

- Is Christ-centered
- Acts as an extension of a church's clearly defined vision
- Is purpose-driven
- Is planned and organized
- Has leaders who are committed followers of Christ and serve as examples to those with whom they work
- Has leaders who feel a sense of calling
- Has leaders who have spiritual gifts that will enable them to effectively lead a ministry
- Has leaders who have received training from a successful ministry from the church, a previous church or from their place of employment
- Is designed to see lives and families transformed by the power of Christ

The chapters in this section will help you develop a focused marriage-building ministry that is designed for success. The overall church ministry and each component of this ministry must have the successful characteristics to be most effective.

chapter three

PURPOSE AND VISION

By the grace God has given me, I laid a foundation as an expert builder, and someone else is building on it.
But each one should be careful how he builds. For no one can lay any foundation
other than the one already laid, which is Jesus Christ.
1 Corinthians 3:10-11

Many are the plans in a man's heart, but it is the LORD's purpose that prevails.
Proverbs 19:21

What is vision? According to Andy Stanley, "Without vision, good things will hinder you from achieving the best things."[1] Simply put, vision is a clear mental picture of what something *could* be, fueled by the conviction that it *should* be.

According to George Barna, "Unless God's people have a clear understanding of where they are headed, the probability of a successful journey is severely limited . . . Realize that true ministry begins with vision. For a Christian leader—that is, an individual chosen by God to move His people forward—vision is not to be regarded as an option. It is the insight that instructs the leader and directs his or her path."[2]

Where does vision come from? Vision for ministry should come from God and should be consistent with His purposes as revealed in the Bible.

Purpose-Driven Ministry

The purpose of something relates to its higher aim or direction. In his book *The Purpose-Driven Church,* Rick Warren asks the thought-provoking question: "What is driving your church?"[3] He then describes several things that can drive a church, including tradition, personality, finances, programs, buildings, events and seekers. He states, "strong churches are built on purpose!"[4] Warren further urges churches to build on a sound foundation just as Paul wrote in 1 Corinthians 3:10: "By the grace God has given me, I laid a foundation as an expert builder, and someone else is building on it. But each one should be careful how he builds. For no one can lay any foundation other than the one already laid, which is Jesus Christ."[5]

Many agree that the following two statements by Jesus summarize what the Church is to be and to do:

The Great Commandment—Matthew 22:37-39
Jesus replied: " 'Love the Lord your God with all your heart and with all your soul and with all your mind.' This is the first and greatest commandment. And the second is like it: 'Love your neighbor as yourself.' "

The Great Commission—Matthew 28:19-20

Therefore go and make disciples of all nations, baptizing them in the name of the Father and of the Son and of the Holy Spirit, and teaching them to obey everything I have commanded you. And surely I am with you always, to the very end of the age.

These two passages give us the primary tasks the Church is to focus on until Christ returns. A purpose-driven church is committed to fulfilling all five Christ-ordained tasks:

1. Love the Lord with all your heart.
2. Love your neighbor as yourself.
3. Make disciples.
4. Baptize disciples.
5. Teach disciples to obey these commands.[6]

As leaders we are challenged to love the Lord with our whole heart, to obey Him and to love our neighbor as ourselves. We are then to make disciples, baptize and teach others to do the same. In a marriage ministry, part of the discipleship process will include teaching couples what the Bible says about relationships, marriage, covenant, communication, etc.

Characteristics of an Effective Purpose Statement

There are four foundational characteristics of an effective purpose statement:

1. **It is biblical**—It is an outgrowth of the Church's purpose as expressed in Matthew 22 and 28. It will also be an outgrowth of other Scriptures as they relate to the particular ministry. (See Genesis 2:21-24; Matthew 19:4-8 and Ephesians 5:21—6:1).
2. **It is simple, clear *and* specific**—Walt Disney's purpose statement was only four words: "To provide people happiness." Remember, "The more you add to your statement, the more diffused it becomes, and the more difficult it is to fulfill."[7]
   "Nothing becomes dynamic until it becomes specific."[8] Go beyond vague statements (e.g., "In our marriage ministry we want to help couples") and specify what exactly it is that you want to help couples do.
3. **It is transferable**—It is short enough to be remembered and communicated to others. People may not remember complete sermons or even paragraphs, but they do remember simple phrases and slogans. Think about some famous people you have seen personally or heard about. Do you remember any speeches they made? How about John F. Kennedy? You may not be able to recount any speech he made, but you probably recognize this well-known statement: "Ask not what your country can do for you—ask what you can do for your country."[9]
4. **It is measurable**—You should be able to look at your statement of purpose and evaluate if your church is doing it or not. Will it be possible to show that you have accomplished it by the end of the year? According to Rick Warren, "Unless it is measurable, your purpose statement is nothing more than a public relations piece."[10]

Your ministry tasks, programs and events can be measured by your statement of purpose. Evaluate your programs with questions such as, Is this program fulfilling the stated purposes of our marriage ministry? and, If it is not fulfilling these purposes, why do we have it?

In writing your ministry purpose and vision statements, look at Scripture passages and God-ordained purposes with your leaders (for a sample purpose and vision statement, see p. 42).

Notes

1. Andy Stanley, *Visioneering* (Sisters, OR: Multnomah Publishers, 1999), p. 12.
2. George Barna, "Power of Vision," *Barna Research Online*. http://www.barna.org/cgi-bin/PageExcerpt.asp?ProductID=8 (accessed February 2003).
3. Rick Warren, *The Purpose-Driven Church* (Grand Rapids, MI: Zondervan Publishing House, 1995), pp. 75-87.
4. Ibid.
5. Ibid.
6. Ibid., pp. 102-106.
7. Ibid., p. 100.
8. Ibid.
9. President John F. Kennedy, "Inaugural Address," *John F. Kennedy Library and Museum,* June 6, 1996. http://www.cs.umb.edu/jfklibrary/j012061.htm (accessed March 6, 2003).
10. Warren, *The Purpose-Driven Church*, p. 101.

Every City Church Marriage Builders Ministry
Purpose and Vision Statement

The purpose of the Every City Church Marriage Builders Ministry is to promote strong marriages and a lower divorce rate by preventing bad marriages, strengthening good marriages, saving troubled marriages and reconciling broken marriages.

We envision a ministry staffed by trained volunteers who are committed to their own covenant marriages and to helping others work toward marriage success.

We envision a ministry that will focus on guiding people to make Jesus Lord of every aspect of their lives.

We envision a ministry in which any couple contemplating marriage can receive counseling and teaching that will prepare them for a successful covenant marriage.

We envision a ministry in which good marriages and troubled marriages will be strengthened by classes, small groups, counseling and retreats.

We envision a ministry where hundreds of couples that are hurting, depressed, frustrated and confused can be led to healing, hope, joy and a renewed covenant marriage.

We envision a ministry that will reach beyond the walls of our own local church to our community.

We envision a ministry where church and community marriages on the verge of divorce will be restored.

We envision a ministry where divorcees will be healed and prepared to be successful in a covenant marriage.

METHODS FOR BUILDING MARRIAGES

Researchers have discovered that marital success is not a matter of luck nor is marital failure a matter of mystery. Using a growing knowledge base, the best practices in marriage education are scientifically based, regularly refined based on ongoing scientific findings and field experience, and have demonstrated beneficial effects in accordance with scientific standards for dissemination.[1]

An effective marriage ministry has strategies for strengthening the relationships of couples in three major groups: those considering marriage, those who are already married and those who are considering divorce, applying sound educational principals in four different arenas: prevention, enrichment, intervention and recovery.

Premarital Preparation

In his book *Marriage Savers: Helping Your Friends and Family Avoid Divorce*, Mike McManus states, "Every church should offer premarital courses for the engaged. The courses should offer substantive help for young couples who want their marriages to be successful. To achieve this goal, churches will have to make a bigger investment of prayer, thought, energy and time to help engaged couples.[2]

It has been said that an ounce of prevention is better than a pound of cure. This is surely the case in marriage ministry! Most often, premarital preparation begins with couples who have already become engaged; however, marriage training should begin with teaching children and youth about how to build strong, healthy marriages. This necessitates cooperation and communication among the children, youth and adult departments in a church.

Premarital preparation for engaged couples may include classes, one-on-one counseling with a staff member, mentoring by a seasoned couple and the completion of a relationship inventory. Premarital preparation for those who have previously been married and then divorced needs to include a divorce recovery class. Classes designed to help divorcees deal with emotional issues from a previous marriage can greatly increase the success of a second marriage.

Mike McManus recommends the following fourfold model of marriage preparation:

1. **Teaching** on the substantive issues of marriage
2. **Equipping** the couple to communicate and resolve conflict
3. **Evangelizing** the couple to help put Christ at the center of their marriage
4. **Helping** each couple learn about marriage via a mentor couple.[3]

A wedding is for a day—a marriage is for a lifetime. It is vital that each couple be taught over and over again that marriage is a covenant that should not be entered into lightly! A one-time emphasis on education about marriage is not enough for couples to fully comprehend the importance of this understanding. Counselors and mentors must continually reiterate this message in order to counteract the worldly if-it-feels-good-do-it mentality portrayed by the media and much of society.

Marriage Policy

Your church will need to develop a clear marriage policy describing requirements for couples wanting to be married at your church facility by a member of the pastoral staff. This policy should describe what type of premarital preparation is necessary, whether the church will marry a non-Christian to a Christian, whether the church will marry a couple that is currently living together, etc. Chapter 11 covers marriage policies in more detail.

Wedding Coordinator

A wedding coordinator can be a great asset to your ministry and can be either a volunteer or paid staff position. Wedding coordinators do just what their job title indicates: they help coordinate many different aspects of the wedding, including verifying the church calendar for open dates, submitting necessary forms for securing a wedding date with the minister and overseeing the couple's progress in fulfilling the requirements of the church in order for the wedding to take place (classes, counseling, etc.) and more.

One wedding coordinator prepared a notebook of information designed to help a young couple in the process of preparing for marriage. It contained fees, florists, church dimensions and available equipment, photographers, music, rehearsal and wedding-day timelines and worksheets, a wedding summary, receptions, maps and parking, forms, etc. The following sample is similar to the first page of that wedding coordinator's notebook:

Preparing for Your Marriage

Applewood Community Church believes that marrying a couple is much more than performing the ceremony. We strongly believe that you should have every opportunity to be prepared for a Christ-centered and biblically grounded marriage—one that is well equipped to exemplify all the Lord intends marriage to be. For these reasons, we ask that you give careful attention to this material and allow sufficient time to complete the premarital process before your wedding. Our prayer is that your marriage will be built on a solid foundation in Christ and serve as a living example of His love for His Bride, the Church.

Your Preliminary Counseling Appointment

Please *do not finalize your wedding date* until you have completed your preliminary counseling session! This is an important opportunity for you and the minister to become better acquainted with each other—and our ministers will agree to marry you only after the completion of this introductory session. (This appointment is also necessary for couples who wish to use the church's facilities and an outside minister.) Please also note the following points:

- Our ministers may not perform ceremonies for couples that are not both Christian.
- Our ministers may perform ceremonies for divorced persons only in the event that the divorce occurred for biblical reasons. (If either of you has previously been married, the minister will want to discuss the circumstances involved in your divorce.)

To schedule your appointment, fill out the enclosed premarital information form and return it to the wedding coordinator, who will review your information and discuss your preferred appointment dates (both you and your partner will need to attend the appointment). Your paperwork will be forwarded to your requested minister's office, and his or her assistant will contact you to arrange your counseling appointment.

The Foundations of Marriage Class

This is a weekend course offered twice a year. Couples being married either here or at another location by one of our ministers are required to attend all classes in this series. We recommend that those being married in the fall take the previous spring class and vice versa. However, every effort will be made to accommodate those who live far away.

The class covers such issues as the biblical foundation for marriage, finances, goals and values, communication, conflict and physical intimacy. Each couple will be asked to complete the premarital assessment. The required fee for this assessment is $50 per couple (this fee covers assessment, materials, lunches and snacks). Scholarships are available upon request.

Each couple in this class will also be paired with a mentor couple that will meet with you at least twice. The mentor couple will be responsible for discussing the results of the assessment with you.

Another item to include in a marriage manual is a class schedule for nearlyweds, similar to the following page:

Nearlyweds Class Schedule

September 8   Topic: Biblical Foundation of Marriage
Welcome and introduction of couples
Introduction of staff

September 15   Topic: P.R.E.P.A.R.E. Inventory
Paperwork and pictures
Notebook overview

September 22   Topic: Communication
Five Languages of Love

September 29   Topic: Conflict Resolution
Luncheon at 12:00 P.M.

October 6   Topic: Communication
Expressive Speaking and Receptive Listening

October 13   Topic: Finances
Money and Your Marriage, part 1

October 20   Topic: Finances
Money and Your Marriage, part 2

October 27   Topic: Intimacy
What the Bible Says About Sex
Food demonstration at 8:45 A.M. (Free recipes!)

November 3   Topic: Intimacy
Helpful Hints for a Happy Honeymoon

November 10   Panel Discussion
Food demonstration at 8:45 A.M. (More free recipes!)

November 17   Topic: Family
In-Laws, Not Outlaws
Brunch at 8:45 A.M.

Premarital Counseling

There are several important elements to premarital counseling. The following guidelines and questions to address while counseling are based on information provided by Frazer Memorial United Methodist Church in Montgomery, Alabama.

Set Specific Goals

Provide Sound Biblical Instruction
1. Does the couple understand the biblical concept of marriage?
2. Does the couple know about and understand biblical principles that will help them succeed in marriage?
3. Has the couple committed to abstinence until their wedding day? Sex before marriage is a sin. If a couple is engaging in sex before the wedding, they will already have a couple of strikes against the spiritual, physical and emotional health of their relationship. If they are willing to repent and then abstain from future sexual intimacy, proceed with the counseling. If not, you should *refuse* to counsel or marry them.

Give an Honest Evaluation
1. Are they compatible (i.e., are they right for each other)?
2. What are the goals and dreams of each individual? Do their goals coincide, or work well together, or are they incompatible?
3. Are both parties Christian?
4. Is God at the center of the relationship?
5. Would you recommend the couple wait to get married or do you feel they are prepared to marry now?
6. What are the primary motivators for the marriage? (Why this person at this time? What outside factors might be influencing the decision to marry?)
7. What do others who know the couple think about their relationship?
8. What problems will each individual bring to the altar (e.g., previous marriages, children, lifestyle issues, money issues)?

Stress That Marriage Is a Lifetime Commitment
1. Will the couple agree that divorce is *not* an option in their marriage?
2. Who will help hold them accountable after the wedding? Who will support them?
3. Does the couple agree that God must be central to their life?
4. Does the couple agree that church involvement is essential? Do they have a church home yet? If not, do they have one they are considering?

Set Specific Guidelines for Premarital Preparation

1. Make premarital counseling mandatory. Churches can—and should—require premarital counseling for all weddings performed at their facility and by their ministers.
2. Make it flexible. Use weekend workshop formats and schedule times that suit both the couple and you.
3. Make it thorough. Because the following topics *must* be covered, each couple will need more than a

single one-hour session. The ideal time period for counseling is 15 to 20 hours—with 8 hours as a bare minimum.

- Spiritual beliefs
- Expectations and roles
- Communication and conflict resolution
- Sex
- Family and friends
- Children and parenting
- Money
- Lifetime commitment versus viewing divorce as an option

4. Make it consistent. Stick to your guns, even when the couples balk at your requirements—allow no exceptions to the rules. Couples will thank you in the long run.

Use Good Resources

There are many resources to help you build your marriage ministry. Ed Wheat, Dennis Rainey, Larry Burkett, Don Meredith and Norman Wright are experts whose writings will provide a wealth of information to help you along the way. (Chapters 15 and 16 of this book contain lists of resources and websites to help you.)

Get Help

Develop Mentors
Couples who have strong Christ-centered marriages and have been married for at least 10 years can be a huge help. Here are some of the advantages to using mentors:

- Decreases your workload
- Adds wisdom and skills to the counseling process
- Encourages growth in a mentoring couple's marriage
- Is another opportunity to include lay involvement in the church
- Builds and strengthens long-term relationships between couples

There is only one disadvantage to using mentors—you will need to spend more time in the short term to train couples to be mentors.

Enlist a Wedding Coordinator
As already mentioned, a wedding coordinator can be a big help. Let's just say it's well worth the effort it takes to get a wedding coordinator program going!

Involve Other Churches in Your Area
Develop a Community Marriage Covenant (see chapter 11 for more information) with as many churches as possible in your geographical area and work with them to offer at least the following:

- Professional premarital seminars and workshops
- Family-life conferences
- Engaged encounter weekends
- Professional counseling centers

Ask for Divine Help

Don't forget to ask God for help! Pray for supernatural discernment and wisdom before you meet with a couple. Take your counseling very seriously; when you do, the couples you counsel will as well.

Always pray with the couples you counsel every time you meet with them and also have them pray in your presence. You gain great insight into a couple's level of spirituality by observing how they handle prayer.

Marital Enrichment

It is important that your church be consistent in its efforts to strengthen marriages. Consider a multifaceted approach that utilizes different time periods, groupings, locations, situations, teachers, counselors and curriculum/book resources to reach a wider group of couples (see chapter 5 for more information).

Marital enrichment topics depend on the age of the couple and the number of years they have been married. You may want to list key issues that married couples encounter at specific life stages and design programs that take those issues into consideration. Topics can include communication, conflict resolution, parenting, life goals, romance, sex, aging, long-term commitment, preventing adultery/infidelity, finances, family mission, etc. The Bible studies in the *Focus on the Family Marriage Series* provide a great foundation for marriages.

Enrichment may also need to include periodic classes and seminars designed to help those who are entering a second marriage and those dealing with the demands of a blended family. In this case it would be wise to utilize as a mentor a seasoned couple that have a successful second marriage. Following is a sample course introduction:

Sample

Community Church's Marriage Course Outline

This four-week course is for any married couple whose desire is to build a strong and lasting relationship. Whether you are newlywed (married fewer than five years) or facing life changes that challenge your marriage (birth of a child, career changes, health issues, empty nest, etc.) or you have been married for a long time and simply desire to renew your marriage, this course will help provide you with the tools you need to renew and rejuvenate your marriage relationship.

During the *Focus on the Family Marriage Series: The Masterpiece Marriage*, we will explore the following topics:

Session One: Great Expectations—God has an eternal purpose for marriage.

Session Two: The Divine Triangle—True happiness and fulfillment in marriage comes from a three-way relationship.

Session Three: The Great Adventure—God gave the first couple work to do, and He provided all they needed.

Session Four: A Walk in the Garden—We can walk with the Lord God in intimate relationship—as individuals and as a couple.

Intervention, Reconciliation and Recovery Ministries

All this is from God, who reconciled us to himself through Christ and gave us the ministry of reconciliation:
that God was reconciling the world to himself in Christ, not counting men's sins against them.
And he has committed to us the message of reconciliation.
2 Corinthians 5:18-20

Intervention

Many churches use mentor couples to help strengthen and enrich marriages in their congregations. Churches that use mentors in their marriage ministry have many success stories of couples whose marriages were saved from the pit of divorce.

Mentoring sessions center around a particular couple's marriage issues. They may begin with a process of marital evaluation. During this evaluation different areas of the relationship are explored, including personality differences, communication, conflict resolution, intimacy, growth, Scripture and prayer. The success of an intervention effort depends on how receptive the couple is to seeking and receiving help and following through on the recommended action.

In addition to mentoring, special classes, intensive counseling and marriage-encounter retreats can be valuable tools for turning these troubled relationships around. There are many organizations that offer marriage retreats throughout the nation (see chapter 16, "Helpful Websites," for more information).

Reconciliation

In his book *The Marriage Reconciliation Conference*, John Cayce writes about the Richland Hills (Texas) Church of Christ's Marriage Reconciliation Ministry and how God has used this ministry to shepherd over 115 dead marriages into new life in Christ. John and his wife, Diane, founded this ministry in 1991 to encourage those struggling with separation, divorce or a seemingly hopeless marriage to trust in God's power and principles to heal and restore their relationships—just as He did for their own marriage.[4]

John and Diane discovered firsthand that God's resurrection power can *and will* resurrect dead or dying marriages from the grave of separation and divorce. Like the apostle Paul, John discovered that the pain and hardship he had been allowed to endure happened so that he would learn to rely not on himself "but on God, who raises the dead" (2 Corinthians 1:9). And it is through their reliance on God that John and Diane have since encouraged countless others in marital conflict to set their hope for the healing and redemption of their marriages.

Let's take a look at Richland Hills Church of Christ's model to see what a successful marriage reconciliation ministry looks like.

The Beliefs
The following are three fundamental beliefs for a successful marriage reconciliation ministry:

- **Matthew 19:26**—All things are possible with God. However, without brokenness in a Christian marriage there can be no mending.
- **Mark 10:1-2**—God intends marriage to be permanent. "God is love" (1 John 4:8,16) and He hates divorce (see Malachi 2:16). When a child of God seeks divorce as a solution, he or she is saying "I cannot forgive" and "God has no power to change my circumstances."

- **1 Corinthians 7:10-11**—It is God's will that broken marriages be reconciled. As Christians we are commissioned to be "ministers of reconciliation" (2 Corinthians 5:18).

The Focus

The main work of the ministry is carried out through weekly support group sessions in which the members share with one another their faith, hope and experiences under the guidance of trained couples—facilitators—who were themselves reconciled after separation and divorce. Love and encouragement from fellow members, daily prayer and Bible study all work together to foster the peace and strength necessary to successfully overcome the circumstances couples face. Members are reminded that God is the ultimate authority in the support group, and facilitators encourage couples to seek solutions for their challenges through Him.

Basic guidelines or rules need to be established to ensure an environment where couples can be vulnerable and trusting with one another.

- Members are asked to commit to at least six to eight meetings before determining whether God, working through the support group, is enabling them to find hope for the reconciliation of their marriage, notwithstanding their present circumstances.

  As members learn to daily surrender their circumstances to God's will and wait on Him, they find that He does meet all their needs, that He uses their circumstances to produce spiritual growth in them and their spouse and that He works for their good which, for most, means the resurrection and healing of an otherwise dead or dying marriage.
- Support-group meetings are confidential. Everything shared must be kept in strictest confidence, including not sharing information on outside prayer lists.
- Neither gossip nor criticism has any place in a support group.

The ministry also sponsors monthly conferences and offers biblically based private or individual counseling.

The Steps

Couples in the ministry learn that there are three steps to reconciliation:

- **Step One—Become reconciled to God.** Before we can expect God to reconcile a marriage, we must first seek to "be reconciled to God" (2 Corinthians 5:20). The potential for reconciling a marriage depends upon our commitment to allow Christ, not only to be our Savior, but also to be our *Lord*—our words, actions and thoughts must all be governed by the Word of God and the Holy Spirit.
- **Step Two—Become reconciled to yourself.** There is a direct correlation between the love and peace we have for ourselves and our ability to show love toward and live in peace with others. We must forgive ourselves for the failures in our marriage and accept the gift of God's unconditional love and forgiveness. Only then can we fully surrender our circumstances to God.
- **Step Three—Become reconciled to your spouse.** Only after we have completed steps one and two will we have the foundation we need to work on becoming reconciled to our spouse. Through practicing the love of Christ in our relationship (see 1 Corinthians 13; Ephesians 5:22-28 and 1 Peter 3:1-7) we can become reconciled to our spouse in the same way that God, through Christ, became reconciled to us—by laying down our life for our spouse (see 1 John 3:16).

Recovery

It is a sad fact that Christians are not immune to divorce. In fact, Christians are divorcing at about the same rate as non-Christians. Your church probably has divorced members in addition to widows and widowers. Divorcees may leave their home church in embarrassment and look for another environment where they can begin afresh. Your church ministry will likely have both new members who left their own churches after their divorce and established members who stayed after their divorce. These members need your help in working through emotional issues connected with their divorce in order to be better prepared, not only to live their lives as singles, but also to be better prepared for possible future marriage.

If your church does not have the necessary resources for developing a divorce-recovery group, research other groups in your area and encourage members to attend these groups.

The nondenominational DivorceCare program is a 13-week program that meets throughout the world in church-sponsored locations. There are two parts to each weekly DivorceCare session. During the first 30 to 40 minutes of the meeting, participants watch a videotape featuring top experts on divorce and recovery topics. These tapes contain valuable information about divorce recovery and are produced in an interesting-to-watch television-magazine format. Following the video, participants spend time discussing the video topic and sharing what's going on in their own lives. Some of the topics covered include emotional, physical and spiritual reactions to divorce; productive steps to take to begin healing; facing anger and depression; dealing with loneliness; new relationships; children; financial issues and forgiveness. For more information on hosting a DivorceCare program at your church or to find a facility hosting one in your area, visit www.divorcecare.org.

Notes

1. Scott M. Stanley, Howard J. Markman and Natalie H. Jenkins, "Marriage Education and Government Policy: Helping Couples Who Choose Marriage Achieve Success," *Smart Marriages,* March 4, 2002. www.smartmarriages.com/choose.marriage.html (accessed November 2002).
2. Mike McManus, *Marriage Savers: Helping Your Friends and Family Avoid Divorce*, rev. ed. (Grand Rapids, MI: Zondervan Publishing House, 1995), p. 128.
3. Ibid., p. 130.
4. John Cayce, *The Marriage Reconciliation Conference* (North Richland Hills, TX: Self-published, 2001), n.p. Used by permission.

CLASSES, SMALL GROUPS, EVENTS AND COUNSELING

In chapter 4 we took a look at the different areas to consider when developing a marriage ministry. In this chapter, we will answer the questions, What form will this ministry take? Where will it take place? What will be the setting? and What will be the approach?

The churches with the most successful marriage ministries use a multifaceted approach that includes classes, small groups, retreats, seminars, conferences, one-on-one counseling and mentoring.

The *Focus on the Family Marriage Series* Bible studies were developed with all of these different venues in mind. They are flexible and easily adapted to any of these situations, and they cover a wide variety of topics to aid in strengthening marriages in your church.

Now let's take a closer look at some of these different approaches.

Classes

Sunday School

Pastors and church leaders nationwide are beginning to rediscover the power of a well-organized and well-staffed Sunday School. In one study, Sunday School was rated as the third highest effective evangelistic methodology.[1] It has also been discovered that "those who were active in Sunday school were five times more likely to remain assimilated in the church than those who were in worship services alone."[2]

A 2001 survey of 353 new Christian adults, showed that 68 percent were active in Sunday School, compared to 58 percent of long-term churchgoers. According to this survey, three major factors were identified as the reason for the new Christians' participation:

1. They had a desire to learn more about the Bible.
2. They were inspired to become involved in ministry through the Sunday School.
3. They enjoyed and sought fellowship with other Christians.[3]

Early in the 1990s Leo and Molly Godzich began a class for young married couples at their church. Just four other couples showed up the first Sunday—today thousands celebrate the covenant of marriage through the ministry of this couple! Today Leo Godzich tells others how to develop a multifaceted safety-net approach to marriage ministry through an organization he founded called National Association of Marriage Enhancement.[4] This approach primarily includes classes, events, mentoring and the influencing of community and state legislation regarding marriage.

Other Venues

Many churches have found it helpful to offer classes during many different time periods in order to serve the largest possible number of people. Classes can be scheduled on midweek evenings or Saturday mornings. Sunday evenings are another option to consider.

Regardless of whether the class is an ongoing weekly Sunday School class or an elective class to last a specific number of weeks, the teacher will have to constantly encourage students to do outside work. Chapter 6 offers insight for structuring classes.

Small Groups

Benefits of Small Groups

There are seven reasons churches need small groups:

1. Small groups encourage spiritual growth.
2. Small groups nourish relational growth.
3. Small groups build emotional support.
4. Small groups stimulate service.
5. Small groups help incorporate newcomers.
6. Small groups develop leadership.
7. Small groups help sustain the Great Commission focus.[5]

Even a large church can have a small, welcoming atmosphere by using the less-formal class approach of small groups. Formal classes feature teaching that generally combines lecture and discussion; small groups use guided discussion as the primary approach. This setting encourages interaction between the participants and helps to create a feeling of belonging and acceptance.

Key Small-Group Values

There are several key values to leading small groups.

- **Affirmation**—It is important to create an atmosphere where group members affirm and encourage one another, build each other up in Christ and help each other grow.
- **Availability**—Time, attention, insight and material resources must be made available to all members in order to meet the needs of and serve one another.
- **Prayer**—Prayer is valued in group life. The group comes together before God to praise, ask, confess and thank the Lord for all He has done. In turn they are humbled, knowing that all comes from God, and encouraged as they see how God answers prayer.
- **Openness**—Reaching the goal of authentic relationship begins with being open with one another.
- **Honesty**—The desire to be honest with each other is critical to authentic relationships (see Ephesians 4:15).
- **Safety**—Honest and open relationships must be guarded with an agreement of safety. Members need to know that what is said in the group will remain confidential and that opinions will be respected and differences will be allowed.

- **Sensitivity**—A commitment to being sensitive to the needs, feelings, backgrounds and current situations of other group members will help build relationships in the group.
- **Accountability**—In authentic relationships, accountability is voluntary submission to other group members for support, encouragement and help in a particular area of life.
- **Evangelism**—As a group, evangelism means being committed to expanding the community of believers through such things as sharing faith, inviting people to the group or other types of contact.
- **Multiplication**—Having the group grow and eventually birth a new group enables each group to carry out the vision of seeing more people connected in Christian community, growing in their relationship with Christ.[6]

Different Types of Groups

There are many different types of small groups. Let's explore just a few.

Bible Study, Fellowship and Prayer Groups

These groups are often extensions of adult Sunday School classes and may meet weekly, bimonthly or once a month. The most popular location for these groups is in the home of one of the group members; and each such group features a host or hostess, a leader and an assistant leader. The hostess sees that the home is prepared for the meetings and arranges for any refreshments; the leader guides the discussion; and the assistant leader aids the leader as needed, even acting as leader when the leader cannot attend. The assistant is generally viewed as a leader in training, and as the group grows it can multiply by sending out the assistant leader to start a new group.

> **Multiplication or Division?** Generally, home-group members have a negative reaction to thoughts of dividing their group, viewing it as separation instead of a necessity due to growth. "Multiplication" of a group is a more positive term for this process.

Bible study, fellowship and prayer groups generally include a time of eating and fellowship, prayer and a Scripture-based discussion. Some Sunday-night groups incorporate the sermon at church that day, extending the sermon's message to allow for interaction and discussion; other groups use discussion-based curriculum. (Of course, the evening discussion can only be a continuation of the Sunday School lesson if that group itself is an outgrowth of the Sunday School class!) These groups become very effective for clarifying biblical truth and discussing how the Sunday-morning message can be practically applied in the lives of the group participants. Often, marriage-focused applications can be made, regardless of whether the original topic was promoted as a marriage topic. After all, the home is the first place that we live out our Christian lives!

Turning Point Ministries uses a wheel to represent a Christ-centered small group. In this wheel, the spokes represent group members and the hub represents Christ. As the group members become closer to the hub—Christ—they also become closer to one another. "Lack of personal growth is often seen in small groups when a group member's problem, the group leader or a philosophy becomes the center."[7] Simply put, placing anyone or anything as the focus or center of a group forms a dependent relationship on that person or thing—and takes away from the focus and dependence we should place on Christ. Heed the instruction provided in 2 Corinthians 1:24 and Colossians 2:8:

> Not that we lord it over your faith, but we work with you for your joy, because it is by faith you stand firm.
> See to it that no one takes you captive through hollow and deceptive philosophy, which depends on human tradition and the basic principles of this world rather than on Christ.

Support Groups

Many church-based small groups are designed for support, but actual support groups have distinguishing characteristics including being led by leaders who are trained to deal with specific issues. These groups are often used by counselors as a part of therapy and are generally designed to help individuals or couples that have unresolved emotional trauma, are in the midst of crises or are dealing with addictions. In this type of group, people feel supported by others who have gone or are going through similar life challenges.

Since crises, emotional issues or addictions that are not dealt with can—and do—lead to divorce, support groups are an important part of a marriage ministry. If an individual church finds it difficult to maintain these support groups along with everything else, it is advisable that they tap in to community support groups or groups offered at other churches. Chapter 4 provides more information on how support groups can be used in marriage reconciliation and divorce recovery.

Accountability Groups

"The distinctiveness of a marriage accountability group is found in the word *accountability*. One of the main reasons for this kind of small group is to hold couples accountable to goals, tasks and plans for their lives and marriages."[8] According to Jeff and Lora Helton, authors of *Authentic Marriages Workbook: How to Connect with Other Couples through a Marriage Accountability Group*, several things are true when you discuss accountability:

- Most people recognize their need for accountability.
- Many people resist accountability.
- Intentional growth and success often happens within accountability structures (exercise programs, diets, etc.)
- Few people have considered using accountability within their marriages.
- Accountability is not a legalistic endeavor.[9]

Further, according to the Heltons, "accountability is what makes a marriage accountability group special. Most Christian couples desire a more intimate and growing marriage; most of these individuals would also recognize the value of accountability in their personal spiritual growth through someone who would disciple or mentor them. We are calling husbands and wives to take those same intentional mentoring and accountability systems and apply them to their marriages. When that occurs, magnificent things can begin to happen."[10]

Retreats, Seminars and Conferences

Accelerated weekend retreats, seminars and conferences are great supplements to your marriage ministry. Some people will find it difficult to regularly attend a course that lasts several weeks, but they will be able to work a weekend of enrichment into their schedule. Speakers also find it easier to commit to weekends rather than several midweek sessions.

Many marriage curricula may be adapted and used for retreat, seminar and conference settings. One of the best-known nationwide marriage retreat programs, Marriage Encounter, was founded in 1962 by Father Gabriel Calvo, a Catholic priest in Spain. This ministry is designed to make good marriages better and strengthen marriages in crisis or at risk. The success rate for these encounters is great—9 out of 10 attendees rate their Marriage Encounter experience very high and indicate that their marriage improved after attending. In a survey of 325 attendees at the beginning of one encounter, only 48 said that they had an excellent marriage; nearly 200 of those same 325 felt that way immediately afterward. This is a 400 percent increase. Today, 100 couples from that same survey rate their marriage as excellent, 145 rate their marriage as very good, and 60 rate their marriage as pretty good. Of the remaining

20 participants, only 10 of the original 325 rate their marriage as the same and the other 10 rate their marriage as rather poor.[11]

Today many marriage-focused organizations conduct national enrichment weekends with very positive results (see chapter 16, "Helpful Websites," for more information on some of these organizations).

Individual Counseling

There are times when it is necessary to refer individuals and couples to a professional counselor. Without professional training, church leaders must tread carefully in the waters of dealing with people who evidence a depth of problems beyond the leader's expertise.

Even good marriages can periodically reach a deadlock and require outside objective help. Marriage is made up of two individuals of different sexes, backgrounds, personalities and expectations. In most cases, there is no bad or wrong person in a relationship difficulty; there are simply two good people who have trouble communicating. Through the process of counseling, these couples can overcome obstacles that hinder them from developing better marriages. It is important that church leaders try to diffuse the negative stigma sometimes attached to professional counseling so that even proud people will be willing to seek help before small problems become big ones.

Social Activities

Planned group social activities are an important part of couple-to-couple fellowship. Phoenix First Assembly in Phoenix, Arizona, calls their in-home dinner groups "Dinners for Eight." Many churches utilize game nights as a way to foster fellowship. Call several churches in your area to get ideas for social activities for your group, and use this special time of fellowship to get to know your group members better!

Notes

1. Thomas S. Rainer, "The Pastor: Key to a Vibrant, Growing Sunday School," *Enrichment Journal*, vol. 7, no. 4 (Fall 2002), p. 18.
2. Ibid., p. 19.
3. Ibid., p. 20.
4. For more information about this organization, visit http://www.nameonline.net.
5. Bill Donahue, *Leading Life-Changing Small Groups* (Grand Rapids, MI: Zondervan Publishing House, 1996), pp. 88-89. Used with permission.
6. Glen Martin and Gary McIntosh, *Creating Community and Deeper Fellowship Through Small Group Ministry* (Nashville, TN: Broadman and Holman Publishing, 1997), pp. 6-10.
7. "Small Groups: A Paradigm for Christian Community," Turning Point Ministries, December 20, 2000. http://www.turningpointministries.org/articles.cfm?fxn=detail&sid=50 (accessed November 8, 2002).
8. Ibid.
9. Jeff and Lora Helton, *Authentic Marriages Workbook: How to Connect with Other Couples Through a Marriage Accountability Group* (Chicago: Moody Press, 1999), p. 23.
10. Ibid.
11. Mike McManus, *Marriage Savers: Helping Your Friends and Family Avoid Divorce*, rev. ed. (Grand Rapids, MI: Zondervan Publishing House, 1995), pp. 174-176.

MENTORING MINISTRY

A firm hired by FamilyLife to help them learn how to better strengthen families recently reported that research determined that those surveyed were in agreement: They wanted a mentor—someone who had already been through their phase of life and could guide them through it. According to Dennis Rainey, this survey revealed that "[People] wanted a real, live person [of] whom they could ask questions—about spanking, about babies' sleeping through the night, about romance and sex, about balancing the demands of work and family, about solving sibling rivalry."[1] Rainey believes that the Church is sitting on an untapped gold mine with two main veins:

1. An enormous number of young married couples would love to have older couples guide them through the formative years of their marriages and families. These couples are young, scared (many come from divorced parents) and *teachable*.
2. An equal number of older married couples need to be challenged to pour their lives into younger couples. But they lack confidence, believing that they have nothing to offer or that their mistakes disqualify them from teaching others.[2]

He also believes that these two groups brought together by the churches will succeed in putting a stop to the culture of divorce prevalent today.[3]

More and more churches are seeing the value of using seasoned couples as mentors for engaged or newlywed couples. A church that adequately uses trained mentors to guide engaged and newlywed couples through specific topics greatly decreases their own premarital counseling load so that they can use their time more effectively. Other churches use mentors with at-risk couples to carry out marriage reconciliation.

Successful Mentoring Ministries

Successful mentoring ministries require careful planning, recruiting, organization, training, communication—you get the idea: Success takes work! Of course, the reward of a well-planned and well-trained mentoring ministry is its positive impact on marriage—and what a blessing that will be! Let's take a look at a few successful mentoring ministries.

Christian Life Center

Dick and Carol Cronk, lay directors of the marriage ministry at the Christian Life Center in Dayton, Ohio, became involved in helping others after experiencing reconciliation in their own marriage through informal mentoring by a coworker and a family member. This mentoring ministry has helped more than 200 couples and, according to Dick Cronk, "When couples call us up and find a listening ear, they'll talk for an hour. It's open to anybody in the community. We usually get several calls a week."[4]

Mentor prospects for the Christian Life Center's program must complete the "Prospective Mentor Couples Questionnaire" (see pp. 121-123 for a sample form). Once approved, couples attend a mentor training weekend program and receive a certificate of completion of the program. Afterward, during a regular church service, the mentor couple will be officially commissioned as mentors by the pastor, who reads sections of the declaration on the certificate and asks the congregation to pray for the couple.

This ministry believes that it is important for the leaders to meet monthly with mentors to plan, problem-solve and provide further training. The following is a letter similar to one sent by the Cronks to the mentors:

Sample

Greetings, Marriage Builder Mentors!

The October Ministry Team Meeting is scheduled for Monday, October 7, 2002, from 6:30 P.M. to 9:00 P.M. at Christian Life Center.

Attendance by all persons involved in ministry is an expectation of the church. Free child care is provided for all attendees.

During the Marriage Builders breakout session, we will hear a presentation on how to mentor and comfort couples who have suffered loss through miscarriage, stillbirth or infant death. You will receive a list of resources that will make a great addition to your mentor-couple resource manual. We will also have on hand a sample of one of the books that the Marriage Builders Ministry provides free of charge to affected couples.

Enclosed is a registration card for a memorial service to be held at CLC on Sunday, October 6, 2002, at 6:00 P.M. If any couples you have mentored have suffered a loss through miscarriage, stillbirth or infant death, please invite them to attend this service and have them fill out the registration card. We have invited two couples we have mentored that have suffered this loss and plan to greet them at the door. Please let us know if you would like to join us there to greet your couple(s).

The evenings of October 6 and 7 will be solemn, exciting and informative. We look forward to seeing you there.

Working for strong marriages,

Dick and Carol Cronk, Lay Directors
Christian Life Center Marriage Builders Ministry

Frazer United Methodist Church

Since the late 1990s, Frazer United Methodist Church in Montgomery, Alabama, has been using seasoned mentors to prepare engaged couples for marriage and to strengthen the marriages of newlyweds. Although the church will marry couples who have participated in other approved premarital preparation, couples are strongly urged to participate in the church's mentoring program as well.

Frazer U.M.C. uses *Preparing for Marriage*, an eight-session program developed by the Family Marriage Ministry of Campus Crusade for Christ. In this program, one or two couples meet once a week for a 90-minute session in the home of a mentoring couple. The weekly sessions combine small-group interaction with video messages. Each week couples are given homework, which takes approximately 45 minutes to complete. They are expected to discuss their homework as a couple before the next week's session. Frazer U.M.C. holds the opinion that the amount of time an individual puts into the study (i.e., homework) is an indication of his or her dedication to building a solid foundation for marriage and also shows how much he or she wants what God desires for the marriage. (The principles taught apply equally to all engaged couples, including those who have experienced a previous marriage.)

The *Preparing for Marriage* course covers the following topics:

- Building a Foundation for Marriage
- God's Plan for Marriage
- Expectations and Roles in Marriage
- Understanding Your Past
- Evaluating Your Relationship
- Communication and Conflict
- Finances
- Preparing for Sexual Intimacy

Marriage Savers

"Is it possible for a church or synagogue to virtually eliminate divorce? Yes, if the congregation trains a network of mentor couples who create a safety net under every marriage," states Mike McManus, founder of Marriage Savers.[5] McManus urges churches to consider the case of the 2,500-member Killearn United Methodist Church in a suburb of Tallahassee, Florida. On the outside, it appears to be a typical large church; however, in the three-year period from 1999 to 2002 the congregation experienced only two divorces—due in large part to its Marriage Savers program.

The National Association of Marriage Enhancement

The National Association of Marriage Enhancement is an outgrowth of the work of Leo and Molly Godzich at Phoenix (Arizona) First Assembly of God. According to Leo, "Divorce has been virtually eliminated from our congregation . . . where some 13,000 people attend worship services every weekend. . . . During the last few years numerous couples have been reunited and even remarried to their original spouses after as many as 11 years of being divorced."[6]

One very important facet of this marriage ministry includes the development of the church's N.A.M.E. Center, which Leo describes as "a place where couples can come to receive couple-to-couple biblical counsel in a confidential and certified manner."[7] Mentor couples are trained to perform basic biblical counseling with the premise that God never intended a senior pastor to spend an inordinate amount of time doing marriage counseling, which could instead be done by trained lay couples whose mentoring could help couples develop strong Christian marriages.

Notes

1. Dennis Rainey, "Mentoring Is Not a Luxury, but a Necessity," *FamilyLife*. http://www.familylife.com/articles/article_detail.asp?id=161 (accessed January 2003).

2. Ibid.

3. Ibid.

4. Dick Cronk, e-mail to author, November 1, 2002.

5. Michael J. McManus, "Marriage Success Stories," *The Morning Call Newspaper*, October 27, 2001, n.p.

6. Leo Godzich, "Challenging the Divorce Culture," *Ministries Today*, (January/February, 2000), n.p.

7. Ibid.

TEACHING FOR LIFE CHANGE

What is learning? Simply put, *learning is change*. When learning has taken place, an individual will demonstrate a changed attitude, idea or behavior—and, often, the person will experience more than one change because these three aspects are interrelated. For example, when what you know about someone changes—perhaps you learn that someone spends every Saturday visiting children in the burn center at the local hospital—your attitude and actions toward that person change. When no change occurs, it indicates there is no learning taking place.

In Christian education, learning is shown through any change that moves a believer toward a deeper relationship with Jesus Christ. In marriage ministry, a participant who moves closer toward conformity with Christ will also become more committed to his or her marriage.

Paul challenged us to change in Romans 12:1-2:

> Therefore, I urge you, brothers, in view of God's mercy, to offer your bodies as living sacrifices, holy and pleasing to God—this is your spiritual act of worship. Do not conform any longer to the pattern of this world, but be transformed by the renewing of your mind. Then you will be able to test and approve what God's will is—his good, pleasing and perfect will.

Now, that's learning!

Creating an Environment of Learning

You can help adults learn even if they do not come to a session or a group expecting to learn. While some learning may occur accidentally, there is much that can be done to increase the likelihood that learning will take place in your group session and in one-on-one mentoring relationships.

So how do you create an environment that leads to learning and finally to change? A good place to begin is by thinking about some of the things that led to changes in your own attitudes and behavior. For example, think of the teacher who had the most positive influence on you. Write down the characteristics of that teacher (e.g., godly, supportive, loving, enthusiastic, encouraging) and also the characteristics of his or her teaching style (e.g., biblical, practical, challenging, down-to-earth, interactive).

To see marriages strengthened through a marriage ministry, you must emulate the characteristics of the teacher whose influence you still fondly remember. This means that you and your workers need to be concerned about who you *are* (your character) and what you *do* (your actions)!

We Teach by Who We *Are*

The old adage "Do as I say, not as I do" is definitely *not* the way to help others learn. Our lives must be consistent with our message; to be an example of what we teach, our heart must be turned toward God. We need to be fully committed to God and allow Him to change *us* before we can help others change. This means we must show that we have a teachable spirit (see Mark 10:35-45; John 13:34; Romans 12:8; Galatians 5:22; 1 Timothy 3:1-7; Titus 1:5-9). But there is more.

In Matthew 16:13-19, Jesus blessed Simon Peter because of his proclamation of faith:

> When Jesus came to the region of Caesarea Philippi, he asked his disciples, "Who do people say the Son of Man is?" They replied, "Some say John the Baptist; others say Elijah; and still others, Jeremiah or one of the prophets."
>
> "But what about you?" he asked. "Who do you say I am?"
>
> Simon Peter answered, "You are the Christ, the Son of the living God."
>
> Jesus replied, "Blessed are you, Simon son of Jonah, for this was not revealed to you by man, but by my Father in heaven. And I tell you that you are Peter, and on this rock I will build my church, and the gates of Hades will not overcome it. I will give you the keys of the kingdom of heaven; whatever you bind on earth will be bound in heaven, and whatever you loose on earth will be loosed in heaven."

It is time to ask ourselves, *What am I building* my *life on*? Jesus is saying to us, "Upon this proclamation of faith I will build your ministry, your family—your *life*." Crucial to your success in a ministry is your answer to the question, *How big is my God?*

We Teach by What We *Do*

Positive results occur when an approach that has been proven to be effective is used. Let's look at some principles related to life-changing teaching.

Pray
When you view yourself as a partner with the Holy Spirit and spend time in prayer, asking for God's strength and guidance, He will provide you with insights and ideas that can effectively communicate the truth of the message we want to teach (see John 14:26).

Know the Goals
In order to change people's lives, you must have a goal for your teaching—a desired result that will occur from what people learn from you. A good curriculum will have three clear goals:

1. **Content**—Group members need to learn biblical content. This framework makes it possible for students to understand messages from specific passages that they can then apply to their lives.
2. **Inspiration**—This goal encourages students to respond emotionally to certain truths from Scripture. In many cases, an appropriate response will include praise or another expression of love for God.
3. **Life-Application**—This goal is to direct students toward maturity, changing their life attitudes and behaviors. As you prepare to teach a lesson, you must think about the way you want group members to apply the principles being taught. Remember: It is only when knowledge moves from the head to the heart that a life is truly changed.

Know the Characteristics and Needs of Your Students

One survey of over 8,000 calls to an outreach phone center found that the most common requests for prayer and help dealt with the following issues, listed in order of frequency:

1. Family relationships
2. Need for life direction
3. Physical ailments
4. Emotional issues (anger, bitterness, peace, etc.)
5. Financial or job issues
6. Addiction (sexual, drugs, alcohol, etc.)

Take some time to find out what your group members are dealing with and what is important to their lives. Lessons that are created with students and their needs in mind will likely be on target. Adults are interested in the immediate application of learning. They want to know "How is this relevant to my life today?" No matter the subject, always provide for the basic human needs, including security, acceptance, love and fulfillment.

Be Real

It is important to create an atmosphere in which it is OK to be human—i.e., imperfect! This means sharing, not only your successes, but also your struggles and mistakes and what you have learned from them. Show others how to apply principles in their lives by demonstrating how those principles have been applied to your life. It is especially helpful when leaders are able to laugh at their weaknesses, making it easier for group members to do the same.

Involve Students

Although lecturing, or delivering a message, is a good method for clarifying and organizing truths, teaching is most effective when students are also involved in the learning process. One way to do this is to provide an outline that students can use for notetaking. Discussion is also an important tool in the discovery process. Through guided discussion, students can discover biblical truth for themselves while still being guided with sound principles of biblical interpretation. This guided discovery helps students take ownership in the learned truth and to use that truth to change their attitudes and behaviors.

Learning Styles

Through all He has created, we can see that God loves variety, and nowhere is this more apparent than in human beings. He purposefully made each one of us a unique creation, from our God-given abilities, gifts and personality to our learning style. Just as our personalities and gifts become the grid through which we see life, our learning style affects how we take in and process information. According to Resources for Ministry, there are four types of learners: visual, auditory, tactile and kinesthetic.[1] Each type of learner has his or her own unique characteristics.

The Visual Learner

Visual learners respond best to lectures that include outlines, graphs, charts, time lines and the like. Because the vast majority of teachers across the United States are visual learners, students are typically taught on the visual track. Visual learners are characterized by the following:

- Learns best when he or she can *see* it
- Likes reading
- Is comfortable with written tests
- Likes to write things down
- Likes visual illustrations
- Likes workbooks and worksheets
- Prefers a quiet and orderly working environment

The Auditory Learner

Auditory learners respond best to large- and small-group discussion, panels, debates, storytelling and the like. Because this group does not like written work or reading, auditory learners are often perceived in classroom environments as not paying attention or not applying themselves. Characteristics of an auditory learner include the following:

- Learns best through verbal interaction
- Prefers to either read aloud or be read to—does not like to read silently
- Likes to listen to tapes and can remember things set to music
- Works better with background sound
- Is not bothered by disorder
- Asks numerous questions to better understand the information
- Does not like written work

The Tactile Learner

Tactile learners respond best to research and projects. As you involved tactile learners in doing things they like (e.g., service projects), they will be more open to learning adaptive skills such as taking notes. Tactile learners share the following characteristics:

- Learns best when he or she can touch
- Likes to fiddle with things
- Likes to take things apart to see how they work
- Learns best with objects he or she can manipulate
- Learns best by doing versus observing or listening
- Needs hands-on learning

The Kinesthetic Learner

Kinesthetic learners respond best to hands-on, multisensory experiences. Because this group learns best when their bodies are in movement, kinesthetic learners are often labeled as having attention deficit disorder or hyperactivity as children. The following characteristics are exhibited by a kinesthetic learner:

- Learns best by doing
- Needs a hands-on approach
- Is motor driven
- Does not do well under bright fluorescent lights

In order to strengthen the marriages in your church ministry, you will need to teach in such a way as to change deeply held attitudes and behaviors. It is important to develop lessons designed for life change!

The Learning Cycle

There is an orderly process by which people learn called the learning cycle. To effectively reach couples in your marriage ministry, you should understand the five phases of the learning cycle, as outlined by author Bobbie Reed in her book *Creative Bible Learning for Adults*.[2]

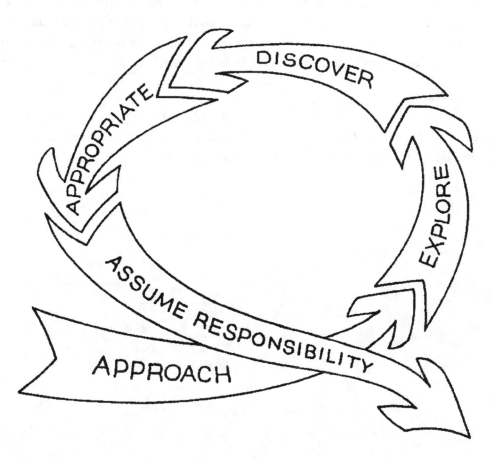

Phase One: Approach
Approach is where curiosity and interest in a subject are aroused. It is the approach that catches someone's attention and draws him or her into the next stages of the process.

For example, let's say you are at the dry cleaner when you see a poster advertising a painting class. You've always wanted to learn how to paint, and you soon find yourself thinking about signing up for a class.

Similarly, in your teaching, you must use an approach that will draw the attention of the students to the topic at hand. To do this, you must plan some ways to cause them to want to learn more about the session topic.

Phase Two: Explore

This is the fact-finding, information-gathering stage of the learning cycle.

In the scenario of wanting to learn how to paint, let's say you sign up for one of the classes. When you arrive at the orientation, you see beautiful watercolors and various painting tools. The instructor explains that well-coordinated paintings utilize various techniques and tools to apply color. Then the instructor patiently guides you through your first brush strokes as you begin to explore the different methods of painting.

Phase Three: Discover

During the process of exploration, we come to a point of discovery. It's as if a light suddenly comes on and reveals what we've been learning in a new way.

In the painting class scenario, let's say you've been practicing your technique and suddenly you realize that utilizing a certain technique creates a desired result. This discovery causes you to want to further explore other techniques to see what else you can learn!

Phase Four: Appropriate

Once we have been involved in exploration and discovery, we are ready to answer the question, *What does this mean to me?* In order to effect a change, we must apply our general discovery to the specifics in our own life.

In the painting class, appropriating means realizing that you don't have to only paint the pictures that the instructor suggests, but now you can design your own pictures by using the techniques you have learned.

Phase Five: Assume Responsibility

After we have explored the material at hand, discovered its meaning and applied discovery to our own life, we must assume personal responsibility to change our behavior in light of what we have learned. Changed behavior is the culmination of the learning process and the proof that learning has taken place.

Notes

1. Resources for Ministry, *Families Under Fire* video series (Fort Worth, TX: Produced in conjunction with the Minirth-Meyer Clinic, 1996).
2. Bobbie Reed, *Creative Bible Learning for Adults* (Ventura, CA: Regal Books, 1997), pp. 48-51.

MINISTRY STAFF

So in Christ we who are many form one body, and each member belongs to all the others. We have different gifts, according to the grace given us. If a man's gift is prophesying, let him use it in proportion to his faith. If it is serving, let him serve; if it is teaching, let him teach; if it is encouraging, let him encourage; if it is contributing to the needs of others, let him give generously; if it is leadership, let him govern diligently; if it is showing mercy, let him do it cheerfully.
Romans 12:5-8

What is the most valuable resource in ministry? Is it the facilities? The curriculum? Actually, it is neither; the most valuable resource in ministry is the *people*.

In Matthew 28:19-20, Jesus commissioned his disciples to "go and make disciples . . . teaching them to obey everything I have commanded." Throughout the New Testament, Jesus made it clear that He expected His disciples to be active in sharing their faith and in teaching others to observe the things He taught them to do. He promised that He would empower His disciples to accomplish this task (see John 14:26-27; 15:26; 16:13-14; Acts 1:8) and that they would have the joy of seeing their faithfulness bear fruit in the lives of others (see John 15:8). Jesus still uses people to accomplish His work!

Gifted for the Task

As David proclaimed in Psalm 139:13-16, each person is a unique combination of personality, natural abilities and experiences:

> For you created my inmost being;
> you knit me together in my mother's womb.
> I praise you because I am fearfully and wonderfully made;
> your works are wonderful,
> I know that full well.
> My frame was not hidden from you
> when I was made in the secret place.
> When I was woven together in the depths of the earth,
> your eyes saw my unformed body.
> All the days ordained for me
> were written in your book
> before one of them came to be.

Scripture also tells us that each believer has been given spiritual gifts. "I wish that all men were as I am. But each man has his own gift from God; one has this gift, another has that" (1 Corinthians 7:7). Ephesians 4:11-13 reaffirms this:

> It was he who gave some to be apostles, some to be prophets, some to be evangelists, and some to be pastors and teachers, to prepare God's people for works of service, so that the body of Christ may be built up until we all reach unity in the faith and in the knowledge of the Son of God and become mature, attaining to the whole measure of the fullness of Christ.

It is important that people are placed in ministries for which they have natural abilities and spiritual gifts and, as Paul pointed out in Ephesians 4:15-16, where they will best serve the Body of Christ:

> We will in all things grow up into him who is the Head, that is, Christ. From him the whole body, joined and held together by every supporting ligament, grows and builds itself up in love, as each part does its work.

Having ministry candidates complete a spiritual-gifts inventory can help them discover their areas of giftedness, which in turn will help you place them in the ministry areas they are best suited for. The Church Growth Institute offers a free online spiritual-gifts inventory at www.churchgrowth.org. The inventory takes about 10 minutes and personalized results are available immediately with no obligation to provide more than the participant's name. The personalized analysis will give the participant a wealth of information, including insights into how to best use his or her gifts. The information provided will be helpful, not only to the person taking the inventory, but also to the leader considering placement of a candidate within a ministry. It's a good idea to include this as a regular part of your newcomers' class.

Qualified Workers

Any person who is to be involved in a teaching, leadership or mentoring capacity must regard the Bible as the authoritative guide to faith and life (see Titus 1:9). These positions require a person of highest personal character and commitment to God, for they will lead by righteous examples of servanthood (see Mark 10:43-45), love (see John 13:34-35) and integrity (see 1 Timothy 3:1-7; Titus 1:6-9).

It is important that teachers, leaders and mentors be spiritually mature individuals. They should have proven themselves faithful in other areas of service and should also complete the church's basic discipleship course. These should be people who are willing to receive training and participate in planning and problem-solving meetings as necessary.

Ask your pastor and other leaders in your church about candidates you are considering. Pray and allow the Holy Spirit to give you guidance in the recruiting process—and listen if your inner guide (the Holy Spirit) says "Wait!"

Responsible Workers

The time to communicate your expectations of those you work with is *before* problems arise. Writing expectations down provides you with an opportunity to organize your thoughts and is a great way to provide clearly stated job descriptions for your ministry workers.

It is generally recommended that a job description include all of the following:

- The date given to the worker
- The position title
- The name of the person to whom the position is responsible
- A brief statement of the purpose and responsibilities of the position

For a valuable ministry resource, check out *The Big Book of Job Descriptions for Ministry* by the Church Growth Institute.[1]

Trained Workers

In the corporate world, individuals with more training are eligible for higher positions and salaries. As procedures change within a company, employees may be required to attend workshops that will enable them to be more effective in their jobs. Typically, the larger the corporation, the more aggressive its training program. How much more we should train people for their work in the church!

In Ephesians 4:11-13, Paul wrote about pastors and teachers and their role in preparing others to do the work of ministry. New and experienced workers alike need to be trained to work within your ministry. It is not wise to assume that once a person has worked in a church ministry, he or she knows how to do the task you have in mind for your particular ministry. Certainly, experienced leaders will be able to build upon knowledge they have learned in previous experiences, but they will still need to receive training that will enable them to be effective in the new task to which they have been called.

A well-trained worker is more likely to be

- Happy
- Patient
- Productive
- Long-term
- In sync with church purposes and vision
- Creative
- Motivated

In general, everyone involved in your marriage ministry will need to be made aware of the ministry's purpose and vision (see chapter 3 for more information on developing ministry purpose and vision). As they see how these relate to the overall church purpose and vision, workers will be motivated to know they are part of something that is bigger than themselves. As previously mentioned, expectations need to be written down in the form of job descriptions. Additionally, workers need to be aware of applicable policies and procedures, and what the ministry goals are for the upcoming months.

Along with a basic orientation, worker training needs to be practical in nature and designed to help develop skills needed to be effective in whatever area of marriage ministry being served.

This book contains many tools to help you train your ministry workers, and following is a list of those tools for three key positions in marriage ministry:

Teachers

- Adult classes (see pp. 53–56)
- Adult characteristics (see pp. 94–100)
- Learning styles (see pp. 65–67)
- Teaching for life change (see p. 63)
- Components of an effective lesson (see pp. 67–68)
- How to lead small groups and adult classes (see pp. 54–56)
- How to encourage discussion (see pp. 101–105)
- The purposes for small groups (see pp. 54–56)

Small-Group Leaders

- Small-group Bible study (see pp. 54–56)
- Adult characteristics (see pp. 94–100)
- Learning styles (see pp. 65–67)
- Teaching for life change (see p. 63)
- How to encourage discussion (see pp. 101–105)
- The purposes for small groups (see pp. 54–56)

Mentors

- Adult characteristics (see pp. 94–100)
- Learning styles (see pp. 65–67)
- Teaching for life change (see p. 63)
- How to encourage discussion (see pp. 101–105)
- Mentoring and counseling relationship (see pp. 57, 59–62)

In chapter 15, you'll find a list of additional resources for training workers, along with a list of other resources that can further enhance your marriage ministry.

Supervised and Supported Workers

If you are over 21 years of age, you have probably served in some capacity as an employee or volunteer. In that capacity, you have either received offensive, inadequate or adequate (effective) supervision. Offensive supervision is very controlling and makes it difficult for you to do your job. Inadequate supervision is typically nonexistent, uncommunicative, uninformative and/or unavailable. Adequate or effective supervision is supportive, communicative, helpful and available.

In addition to careful orientation and training, adequate supervision and guidance can prevent most problems. Workers need to feel there is someone to go to for help, and to be encouraged when they ask for that help, whether the help is in the form of problem solving, ideas or just support. Workers should never be recruited and then forgotten—unless you want failure in the ministry. Effective supervision also sees that workers are provided with supplies, curriculum, equipment and facilities as needed.

No matter your method—regular mail, e-mail, telephone, personal contact or group meetings—the importance of clear communication cannot be overemphasized!

Phone Conversations

Phone calls may be used to follow up written communications, deal with problems, encourage and recruit. Make your phone calls pleasant and brief, but be sure they are long enough to accomplish their goal.

Regular Mail and E-Mail

Although e-mail has become a very popular mode of written communication, you will find that some people do not have access to a computer or do not have an e-mail address. Or you may prefer writing notes yourself and mailing them the old-fashioned way. Regardless of the mode you choose for sharing written communication, here are some helpful hints:

- Include a warm greeting and an expression of gratitude for their commitment to the marriage ministry.
- Make your communication brief, specific and to the point.
- Organize the correspondence in a logical fashion, placing the more important items at the beginning or end of the list.
- Highlight key points (use <u>underline</u> if notes are handwritten or **bold** if typing) so that they will not be overlooked.
- Use a warm closing.

A note about e-mail: If you have a lot of information to communicate in an e-mail, consider sending it in two or three short topic-specific notes instead of one larger multitopic one.

Personal Contact

Personal contact is an extremely important format for communicating. All personal contact should be warm, affirming and encouraging. It should allow the worker opportunity to express concerns and work out problems, if necessary. Be sure to meet personally with your key ministry leaders.

Group Meetings

Leaders are encouraged to meet on a monthly basis with key workers. Meetings must be well organized. Be careful to not waste workers' time with rambling speech or meaningless chatter. Meetings should include prayer, group problem solving, planning and/or training tips, any communication concerning anything that affects workers (e.g., changes in policies or procedures, calendar events or changes in leadership).

In general, plan meetings to be warm, inspirational, practical and convenient; and workers will be more likely to be faithful in attending. One final note: Be sure to arrange for child care for workers who have young children, so those workers are not left out. (See chapter 9 for more information on planning meetings.)

Motivated Workers

Motivation is the key to a ministry functioning at its highest level of effectiveness. The more you develop your ability to motivate ministry workers, the more effective the overall ministry will be.

Share the Big Picture

One way in which people become motivated is through an understanding that they are an important part of something that is bigger than they are. The bigger-than-me aspect of motivation relates to the concept of how an individual's participation in a ministry relates to the purpose and goals of the church as a whole.

Offer Opportunities for Achievement

People want to be involved in activities in which they can achieve success. The opportunity to succeed is a huge motivator and the key to this is the placement of people in the ministry areas for which they are best suited.

Emphasize the Goals

Most people place a high importance on achieving goals and enjoy the idea of having something to work toward. Goals provide a basis for evaluation, feedback and decision making. As a leader, your role is to be aware of and effectively remove any obstacles that prevent your ministry workers from achieving their goals.

Recognize a Job Well Done

Even more than material incentives, most people want proper recognition when their job is well done; this is especially true for volunteers. Let's face it: Ministry isn't easy. Workers who feel they are respected, honored and recognized for their ministry involvement—whether from leaders, students or peers—will be more inclined to go far beyond the call of duty in fulfilling their ministry responsibilities.

Provide Ample Support and Guidance

Workers need to know that they are not alone in their work and that support and guidance are readily available. Proper supervision will provide support and guidance for all workers, from the newly trained to the seasoned volunteers.

Show Acceptance and Respect

People of all ages and walks of life thrive on acceptance, not for what they do, but for who they are. This type of acceptance says "I accept you in spite of your imperfections because I am not perfect either."

People also want respect for their abilities, opinions and time. Respect for a ministry worker is shown in many ways, including the following:

- Make requests, not demands.
- Ask for suggestions when problem solving or planning special events.
- Make eye contact when talking *and* when listening.
- Allow others to finish talking before you offer your comments or suggestions.

These are just a few of the more important aspects of motivating others. Luke 6:31 says it all: "Do to others as you would have them do to you."

Note

1. Church Growth Institute, *The Big Book of Job Descriptions for Ministry* (Ventura, CA: Gospel Light, 2002).

PLANNING AND ORGANIZATION

The seven years of abundance in Egypt came to an end, and the seven years of famine began, just as Joseph had said.
There was famine in all the other lands, but in the whole land of Egypt there was food.
Genesis 41:53-54

The story of Joseph's preparing Egypt for famine is just one biblical example of planning and organization. What Joseph attempted was no easy task; it required thought, foresight and prayer. In the same way, a successful and effective ministry takes careful planning and organization *and* prayer!

Developing a Master Plan

According to Turning Point Ministries, one of the greatest obstacles to a successful small-group ministry is a start-and-stop approach.

> In the start-and-stop approach, completion of small group study is seen as an end in itself. In other words, the emphasis of the ministry is on starting up a small group that will meet together for a certain number of weeks. Then, when the small group study is completed, the ministry "shuts down" until the next small group is ready to be organized. The obstacle this approach presents is stagnation. Time and energy . . . is spent "reinventing the wheel," performing the same start-up functions at irregular intervals. . . . Three elements are necessary for implementing a "process" mindset in the ministry: a master plan, continuous new leadership training, and communication.[1]

Important Elements in a Master Plan

It Must Be Ministry Specific
The master plan must be in tune with the specifics of the ministry. When drawing up your plan, be sure to include the number of leaders and ministry workers who will be participating in the ministry. Also include the church calendar schedule in your planning.

It Must Be Detailed
Your plan should define the ministry policies and procedures. It should be comprehensive and detailed, covering topics such as what should be done if a leader cannot attend a scheduled meeting; how and when new leaders should be trained; how to promote your ministry; options for small groups, etc. Every contingency you can think of should be covered in the ministry's master plan. (See chapter 2 for more information on policies and procedures.)

It Must Be Flexible

As detailed and comprehensive as your plan should be, it is impossible to predict everything that might occur within the ministry. "Provisions and alternatives should be built into the plan to account for the natural processes of turnover and attrition. By the same token, flexibility in the plan will allow ministry leaders to take advantage of opportunities that arise."[2]

Establishing Staff Relationships

It is always helpful to lay out the organizational structure of your ministry's chain of command in the form of a flow chart. This provides a visual description of the ministry relationships and will prove helpful for visual learners. (For more information on learning styles, see chapter 7.) In addition to the flow chart, it is important to indicate on each position's job description the person to whom that position is responsible and to whom questions or concerns should be addressed.

As members of the marriage ministry team, your common goal is to strengthen the marriages in your church. Although each member of the team will have specific responsibilities, it's important not to lose sight of the fact that you are a team. An important way to keep a team spirit is to hold team meetings on a regular basis—at least monthly.

Team meetings should be scheduled well in advance, and attendance should be required of all team members. As a side note, be sure to include this requirement in each team position's job description. It will be a sacrifice of time for team members to attend these meetings, so it is important that the meetings be worthwhile and include a time of comfort, encouragement and bonding so that attendees will look forward to the next meeting. One way to ensure the meeting will be beneficial is to have an agenda. Using an agenda to provide structure for meetings will help you complete what you need to accomplish in the allotted time. An agenda should include all of the following:

- A time of encouragement and Scripture reading
- Updates, progress reports, praise reports
- Areas of general concern
- A training nugget or helpful teaching tip
- Time for problem solving and prayer

Vital Elements for Your Marriage Ministry

There are three major elements for a successful marriage ministry.

Pastoral Support

Pastoral support is crucial to a church's marriage ministry. Not only must the pastor be behind the ministry, but he or she must also make this support known publicly. Pastoral pulpit announcements and comments can reinforce your ministry's legitimacy and value to the congregation.

It would be beneficial to ask your pastor to attend the initial leadership meeting. If he or she cannot attend this meeting, be sure that the key ministry leader meets with the pastor to communicate in detail the ministry's purpose and agenda. This key leader should continue to keep the pastor informed of the ministry's progress. In this way, the pastor can feel a part of these successes and will continue to support the ministry. And don't forget to point out that a successful marriage ministry can significantly lighten a pastor's marriage-counseling load!

Qualified Lay Leadership

Leadership is a key component to any ministry success. Successful leaders are qualified, gifted, called, equipped and motivated by their love for God and His people.

Successful Integration

Your church's new marriage ministry must be incorporated into the larger church body. This begins with the pastoral announcements from the pulpit and extends to include staff members from other ministries within the church in the process of brainstorming ideas for the marriage ministry.

Notes

1. "Keeping Momentum in Your Turning Point Ministry," *Turning Point Ministries*, March 2, 2001. http://www.turningpointministries.org (accessed November 8, 2002).
2. Ibid.

MARRIAGE MINISTRY AND EVANGELISM

Therefore go and make disciples of all nations, baptizing them in the name of the Father and of the Son and of the Holy Spirit, and teaching them to obey everything I have commanded you.
Matthew 28:19-20

The following is a true story:

The wedding coordinator at Park Cities Presbyterian Church in Dallas listened as the mother made her request. Carefully, the mother explained that her teenage son wanted to get married in the church and asked about the requirements. The coordinator told her that either she or one of the engaged would need to be church members. This requirement being met, the coordinator listened as the mother explained that her son's fiancée was pregnant! The coordinator began the process by getting other necessary information from the mother and putting in a request for this couple to meet with a pastoral counselor. The couple would need to be willing to complete the church's Foundations of Marriage course and receive the approval of this counselor before they would be assigned a date on the church calendar.

The young couple talked to the counselor about their desire to marry. Concerned with their spiritual condition, the counselor asked pertinent questions. Determining from their answers that they were not in right relationship to God, he began to guide them gently, presenting Scriptures. He encouraged them to make Christ the foundation of their marriage. One seemed on the brink of a life-changing commitment, while the other held back. Wanting to allow the Lord time to work, the counselor gave the young couple some material to read and made an appointment for them to meet with a mentor couple two weeks from that date.

After the two weeks had passed, the couple met with the mentor couple. The one who had held back on making a commitment to Christ had softened. The Lord had been working in both of their hearts, and the mentor couple prayed with them as the young couple accepted Jesus as their Savior and Lord. This was their first step toward a well-founded marriage—and, in the words of the wedding coordinator, "They have married and are now growing in the Lord!"

Park Cities Presbyterian Church in Dallas, Texas, views its marriage ministry as an opportunity to change lives as the ministry works with couples who are considering marriage. In every meeting, counseling and mentoring session, the love of Christ is shared, pointing to a commitment to Him as the foundation of a solid marriage. This evangelistic emphasis is probably one of the main reasons P.C.P.C. has grown to 6,000 members in only 12 years!

Your church's marriage ministry, like that of P.C.P.C., has a tremendous opportunity to reach couples for Christ. As a marriage ministry leader, you will have the following opportunities, among others:

- Lay a solid biblical foundation upon which young couples can build their marriage.
- Help couples develop skills that will strengthen their marriages.
- Be an instrument of Christ's healing grace in the lives of hurting believers.
- Be an instrument of Christ's healing grace in the lives of unbelievers.

A Common Concern

Both Christians and non-Christians care about their marriages. A marriage ministry has the unique opportunity to bring into the church the very same people who might otherwise never step foot in a church. Marriage ministry leaders have the unique opportunity to share with these people what life in Christ can do. Leaders should be prepared for such opportunities and should look for nonthreatening ways to share aspects of the Christian life with non-Christian group members.

According to researcher George Barna, the majority of non-Christians are interested in spiritual matters, shown by the fact that most of them have some form of personal involvement in religious communications or development. Even one out of four unchurched people will read the Bible during a typical month. "The same proportion is engaged in reading a religious book or magazine and in watching a religious television program during a typical month. One out of five [unchurched] adults listens to a religious radio program during the month. And 7 out of 10 pray to God each month."[1]

It is important that the Church press the hot buttons that will draw in the unchurched. "Like it or not, the [unchurched] population is perhaps most open to religion if it can help solve some of their problems or address some of their most pressing needs."[2]

Many married couples don't seek help when their marriage is in crisis. Is this because they don't want help? No. Many times it is because professional therapy is too costly. Your church can offer minimal-cost or even free counseling to help get their marriage back on track while helping them to develop an intimate relationship with God.

Promoting Your Ministry

Chapter 14 contains ideas to help you promote the marriage ministry, both inside and outside your church. You'll find sample flyers, brochures and posters that you can adapt for your own use—but don't forget: *The* most effective means of getting people into the church is through personal invitation. This is especially true of the unchurched. The unchurched are more likely to participate in a marriage ministry if invited or brought by a trusted friend. "Surveys and market testing of other approaches have shown that nothing compares with the effectiveness of the personal touch."[3]

Surveys have shown that there are two strategies for approaching the unchurched about coming to church that are appealing to them:

1. **Caring, Honest Relationships**—The unchurched respond positively to invitations from caring, honest friends who attend church.
2. **Nonreligious Events**—Events that are not overtly religious are viewed as safe by the unchurched. They can come to a nonreligious event and enjoy the activities without feeling pressured to join the church. When the church sponsors nonreligious events—such as sports leagues, community

fairs, social extravaganzas, community assistance projects and concerts or seminars of interest to the unchurched—leaders can use the opportunity to extend an open invitation for attendees to come back for a church service and to check out the different ministries the church offers.[4]

Likewise, there are two strategies to avoid at all costs! Both of these strategies send the message that a church's agenda is more important than an individual's privacy and time:

1. **Telemarketing**—Calling people on the phone who don't know you to invite them to church leaves a bad taste in the mouths of the nonchurched.
2. **Uninvited Visitation**—Not many people enjoy uninvited visitations from strangers. "This creates a measurable hostility toward the Christian faith and its churches."[5]

Notes
1. George Barna, *Evangelism That Works* (Ventura, CA: Regal Books, 1995), p. 52.
2. Ibid., p. 54.
3. Ibid., pp. 54-55.
4. Ibid., p. 63.
5. Ibid.

One-Verse Evangelism®

An Easy Approach to Sharing the Gospel

The gospel is most powerful when shared simply and with love. This approach is a simple, interactive way to share Christ's love visually and conversationally. It utilizes questions and sharing, and because it uses just one verse, it can be presented in less than 15 minutes. Here is how One-Verse Evangelism works.

Let's imagine that you are counseling or mentoring a young couple who has decided to marry. After conversing with them for a few minutes, you are unsure whether or not the man and woman are Christians.

Approaching the subject of building a solid foundation for marriage, you begin to talk to the couple about the importance of having a three-way in partnership marriage, with God at the top. As you are talking, you write out Romans 6:23 on a piece of paper: "For the wages of sin is death, but the gift of God is eternal life in Christ Jesus our Lord." When you are done, you offer to show the couple a simple illustration of God's relationship with His people.

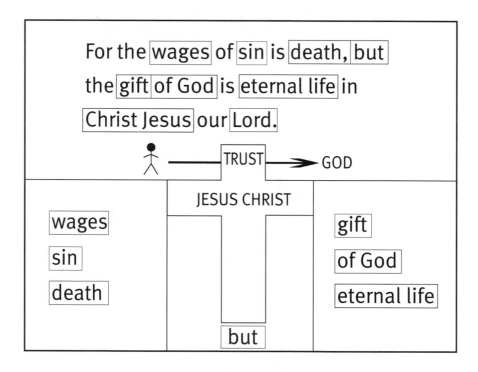

The text on the following pages explains how to talk through the process as you draw the diagram.

Wages

Circle this word and ask, "How would you feel if your boss refused to pay you the wages that were due to you?" Deep down, we all know that it is only right that we get what we deserve. Similarly, we earn wages from God for how we have lived our lives.

Sin

Draw a circle around "sin," asking your friend what he thinks when he hears this word. You might explain that sin is more an attitude than an action. It can be either actively fighting God or merely excluding Him from our lives. You can ask, "Has God ever seemed far away?" If he says "Yes," add that that's one of the things sin does—it makes God seem far away. Now draw two opposing cliffs with a gap in between.

Death

Circle this word and ask what thoughts come to mind. Explain that death in the Bible always means some kind of separation.

But

While circling the word, mention that it is important because it means that a sharp contrast in thought is coming. What we have just looked at is bad news; what follows is good news.

Gift

Draw a circle around this word. Ask, "If wages are what a person earns, then what's a gift?" Remind your friend that someone must purchase every gift.

Of God

Circle this and explain that the gift you are talking about is free. It is from God Himself. It's so special that no one else can give it. Ask, "How do you feel when someone gives you a special gift?"

Eternal Life

Circle these two words next and then ask, "How would you define these words?" Contrast one side of the cliff, death, with the other side, eternal life. Ask, "What is the opposite of separation from God?"

Jesus Christ

Draw these words so they create a bridge between the two cliffs. Help your friend to consider that every gift has a giver, and only Jesus Christ can give the gift of eternal life.

Trust

Write this word over the bridge you just drew. Explain that friends trust each other, and tell your friend that Jesus wants a trusting friendship with him. All he has to do is admit that he is responsible for the "sin" of either fighting or excluding God from his life. That is what trust means—trusting that Jesus wants to forgive us for rejecting Him from our lives. At this point, you can ask him if he wants to start a relationship with God that will last forever. If he says "Yes," invite him to pray a short prayer in his own words, asking Jesus to forgive him.

Close by reminding the person that this simple illustration shows what God is like: Someone who really cares about people, especially him or her. Invite him or her to read all about it in the Bible, perhaps beginning in the gospel of John.

Adapted with permission from One-Verse Evangelism, © 2000 Randy D. Raysbrook. To order booklets containing the complete version, please contact Dawson Media c/o The Navigators, P.O. Box 6000, Colorado Springs, CO 80934.

NATIONAL AND COMMUNITY MARRIAGE MOVEMENTS

Over the past few years God has been raising up religious leaders, politicians, educators, counselors, statisticians, social scientists and others to affirm the importance of establishing and maintaining wholesome marriage relationships. The effectiveness of your marriage ministry can be enhanced by combining forces with national and community marriage movements.

Covenant-Marriage Contracts

Legally, covenant marriage laws generally allow a couple to choose to have slightly more limited grounds for no-fault divorce in their marriage. The couple is required to go through marriage education or counseling before they marry (or for those already married, before the conversion of their current marriage to a covenant marriage). A covenant marriage also requires that a couple attends counseling—and sometimes a two-year waiting period during which the couple will receive counseling for reconciliation—before divorcing. In some states, the couple further agrees that divorce is not an option unless due to adultery, abuse or abandonment.

Legally Binding Covenant-Marriage Contracts

Legal covenant marriages are currently available only in Arizona, Arkansas and Louisiana. However Georgia, Oklahoma, Oregon and Texas are also seeking to pass legislation making such marriages legal. In most states you do not have to be a state resident to get married in the state or to convert an existing marriage into a covenant marriage.

To view an actual covenant-marriage law—passed by the state of Louisiana—visit http://patriot.net/~crouch/cov/index.html.

Nongovernmental Covenant-Marriage Contracts

The concept of covenant marriage began, not as legislation, but instead as a way of teaching people to renew and strengthen their marriages. The Covenant Marriage Movement offers covenant-marriage documents that serve as social, moral and spiritual contracts rather than legal ones.

Marriage Movements

Americans for Divorce Reform

The Americans for Divorce Reform website offers a wealth of valuable information on the latest legislation, news, opinions and scholarly articles on the subject of covenant marriage, including related proposals for choice in marriage and divorce. For more information, visit their website at www.divorcereform.org/cov.html.

The Covenant Marriage Movement

On February 23, 1999, a meeting was held in Dallas, Texas, to introduce the Covenant Marriage Movement to representatives from 19 church and parachurch ministries and organizations. There was a unanimous decision on the part of these ministries to encourage their respective ministry or organization to support the Covenant Marriage Movement, which was then officially announced on May 11, 1999.

Currently over 50 large organizations have aligned themselves with the movement, including the American Association of Christian Counselors, Assemblies of God, Christian Broadcast Network, Christian Financial Concepts, Inc., Christian Men's Network, FamilyLife, Focus on the Family, Friends of the Family, LifeWay Christian Resources, Living Way Ministries, Moody Bible Institute, National Association of Marriage Enhancement, Promise Keepers, Smalley Relationship Center, Southern Baptist Association of Counselors and Family Ministers, and others.

For more information, visit www.covenantmarriage.com.

Marriage Savers

Founded in 1996 by Mike and Harriet McManus, Marriage Savers is a ministry whose goal is to lower divorce rates by equipping local congregations to help couples prepare for, strengthen and restore marriage. The key strategy is for local clergy to adopt a Community Marriage Policy®, in which clergy agree to train couples to mentor other couples.

The adoption of the first Community Marriage Policy in 1986 by the city of Modesto, California, has directly resulted in a 48 percent decline in the divorce rate for that city—and an increase in the marriage rate of 14 percent, while the marriage rate in the United States declined by 18 percent during the same period! Over 155 more cities have adopted the policy thus far; and cities such as Baton Rouge, Louisiana; Tallahassee, Florida; and Columbus, Georgia; have seen a 6 percent decline in divorce rates in just the first year the policy was adopted. Other cities have had much more dramatic plunges in the divorce rate: 22 percent in Peoria, Illinois; 31 percent in El Paso, Texas; and 44 percent in Kansas City, Kansas.[1]

The following Community Marriage Policy was signed by 64 pastors on January 15, 1999 in Tallahassee, Florida, and was praised as a model for Florida by newly elected Governor Jeb Bush.[2]

Tallahassee Community Marriage Policy*

We Believe

- That God has established in Scripture the sanctity and companionship of marriage;
- That God intends the marriage bond between husband and wife to last a lifetime;
- That as church leaders we have a responsibility to provide premarital preparation to every engaged couple. This will improve their understanding of marriage and deepen their mutual commitment;
- That as clergy we have a responsibility to provide ongoing support to strengthen and nourish existing marriages.

Therefore, We Will

- Encourage a courtship of at least one year;
- Expect a minimum of five counseling sessions for engaged couples, preferably over a 3- to 4-month period, with one session devoted to taking a premarital test or inventory; one devoted to ensuring a biblical understanding of morality, marriage, and divorce; and one devoted to a postmarriage follow-up;
- Train mature married couples to serve as mentors to those who are engaged, newly married, experiencing marriage difficulties or remarried;
- Encourage retreats, classes and marriage-enrichment opportunities designed to build and strengthen marriages;
- Develop and implement programs for troubled marriages using counseling, retreats and mentoring by couples (including those whose own marriages were once in trouble);
- Promote sexual abstinence outside of marriage;
- Promote faithful marital relationships;
- Set an example as pastors by attending couples' retreats and being involved in other relationship enrichment activities;
- Take this covenant back to our church to be ratified by the appropriate church leadership.

* Sponsored by *Live the Life Ministries* locally and *Marriage Savers* nationally.

The Colorado Marriage Project

The Colorado Marriage Project, or CMP, fights divorce by providing resources and information regarding marriage mentoring, premarital counseling and community marriage standards. Its goal is to "create a Community Marriage Agreement in every city in Colorado."[3]

The heart of the Colorado Marriage Project is its Community Steering Committees (community-based groups of local clergy). The focus of these committees is to produce and sustain a community marriage agreement for their city or county. Setting up a marriage project for your city is a four-step process which includes

1. Setting up an informational meeting to introduce your marriage project;
2. Forming a Community Steering Committee of local clergy;
3. Forming a Community Marriage Agreement; and
4. Completing the Community Marriage Agreement.

The Rocky Mountain Family Council offers a Community Marriage Agreement brochure that includes an outline of the vision and goals of the Colorado Marriage Project. You can get this brochure by contacting the Rocky Mountain Family Council at 303-292-1800.

For downloadable sample church policies and more information on setting up your community's steering committee and Community Marriage Agreement, visit www.marriageproject.com.

What Churches Can Do

A marriage-covenant congregation is one that commits to providing a ministry to married couples who are members of their congregation or who are planning to be married within their congregation based on the Covenant Marriage Vow.

The Church's Responsibility

When a married couple is united with the congregation, the congregation is entering into a covenant relationship with that couple and the couple's family. That covenant, initiated by the congregation, is one that comes from God and is lived through the local body of Christ. Therefore, each local congregation, in obedience to the covenant given to them by God, has the responsibility to love that couple as Christ Himself loves the Church. Not only are God's people to be *keepers* of the covenant, we are to be *participants* as well.

Marriage Preparation

Marriage preparation includes the following:

- A study of Scripture related to marriage and the covenant
- Administration of a marriage preparation inventory to help couples identify and discuss relationship strengths and growth areas that may need to be addressed prior to marriage
- Six sessions with an authorized marriage preparation couple or minister of the organization
- A commitment to unite with a newly married or young married couples class whose focus is on enriching or enhancing God's gift of marriage

As a covenant-marriage congregation, will you offer the ministries to couples in your congregation and community? Some of the most valuable time spent in the ministry will be spent with couples preparing for and living in a covenant-marriage relationship. In addition to what you can do with your staff, you can equip lay couples to assist you in carrying out these recommendations. The following are some actions you can take, as suggested by the Covenant Marriage Movement:

- As a congregation, establish and affirm an intentional marriage policy. This policy must focus on the couple, their relationship and the congregation's commitment to their marriage.
- Provide at least six marriage-preparation sessions and two follow-up sessions during the first year of marriage.
- Provide an annual sermon series on marriage/family relationships. The focus of these messages should be on biblical teachings and life applications for establishing and enhancing relationships and building strong, growing Christian families. They should also provide a biblical understanding of covenant and how it applies to marriage and family.
- Provide media resources such as books, magazines, tapes, videos and interactive learning resources. These resources can be checked out and/or purchased.
- Provide at least one biannual marriage-enrichment retreat. This should be an overnight experience for couples only. Focus on relationship enhancement, skill development and spiritual renewal.
- Pair up newly married couples with older covenant couples for the purpose of providing guidance for a period of two years.
- Provide at least one annual Covenant Marriage Commitment service where couples have an opportunity to publicly affirm their marriage as a covenant relationship.

Notes

1. For more information and statistics, visit www.marriagesavers.com.
2. Mike McManus, "The New Politics: Saving Marriages," *Ethics and Religion*. http://www.marriagesavers.com/Columns/C908.htm (accessed January 2003).
3. "Community Group Formation," *The Colorado Marriage Project*. http://www.marriageproject.org/comgroup.html (accessed January 2003).

building tools

WORKER TRAINING MATERIALS

This chapter contains some valuable tools for teaching ministry staff. Should you utilize any of these handouts for worker training, we urge you to do more than copy the material and pass it out. Carefully go over each point with your workers and allow them to discuss it and ask questions. After reviewing the material with them, you may want to ask, "How will this affect the way you minister in your situation?" This will encourage them to apply the principles they learn as they carry out their own ministries. In some cases you might find it helpful to include a role-play activity that illustrates how the principles may be applied in a small-group situation.

Distinctives of Adult Learning

- **Some of the adults that come to your class do not come with a *learner's attitude*.** If the teacher exemplifies a learner's attitude, it is more likely that the students will develop one.

- **Adults come with *definite ideas*.** As a person ages, personality and beliefs become more rigid. They are resistant to change unless they see that what is being offered in the class is related to their everyday lives and promises to make them more productive.

- **Adults come with *more experience* than young people.** They have had a greater exposure to ideas and experiences. They will respond positively if they see that you respect their experience. They have much to contribute to the learning experience and may feel thwarted if they are not allowed to participate and learn from one another as well as from you.

- **Adults are accustomed to the *immediate application of learning*.** They want to know, "How is this relevant to my life? Does this Bible lesson offer me anything now? I have some needs and problems that must be satisfied now. Will this really work?"

- **Adult involvement in learning is *basically voluntary*.** The needs of the adults and attractiveness of the course offered must be united.

- **Some adults have a tendency to be *apprehensive in learning situations*.** This can affect the progress of the class and individual. Apprehensive adults will not easily open up and share personal information or ask questions. They are afraid of revealing areas of ignorance. They want to feel responsible and in control at all times. They are somewhat intimidated by situations in which their self-image is threatened. They may also be fearful of potential disagreements, which might cause pain unless there is an open and accepting atmosphere.

- **Adults learn through their *own efforts*.** They can be guided, encouraged, excited and motivated by an outside force, but they must do the actual changing. This change occurs when they do something—discuss, think, debate, practice. They must internalize the material so that it becomes their own.

- **Adults learn by their *identification with groups*.** If people attach themselves to a certain group, they have done so for a specific reason. They like to be with the people in that group, or the group has something to offer them. Adults enjoy learning with people with whom they feel at ease.

- **Adults learn from the *example* of the teacher.** Teachers must be the kind of people they want their learners to be. Research indicates that when people teach one thing and model something else, the teaching is much less effective than if they were to practice what they teach.

- ***Feedback* is very important for adults.** Learners need an opportunity to find out how they are doing. Provide opportunities for your adults to share what they have learned.

- **Adults come into a learning situation with more *pressures and responsibility* than young people.** If they come to a study program in the evening after a hard day's work, they are often fatigued. Timing, therefore, is important in planning an adult enrichment program.

- **Teachers must rely on the *Holy Spirit* to bring about change.** The Holy Spirit can bring about changes in the learner's understanding, attitudes, values, motives and behavior.[1]

Note

1. Bobbie Reed, *Creative Bible Learning for Adults* (Ventura, CA: Regal Books, 1977), pp. 49-50.

Getting to Know Busters*
(People Born Between 1963-1977)

Important Facts

- 72.2 million in this generation
- First generation born after The Pill was introduced
- Many latchkey kids
- Educated in the chaos of open classrooms and new math curricula
- Raised amidst an information explosion, the emergence of a global community, the end of the Cold War, the emergence of AIDS, corporate downsizing, decreasing income, and increasing cohabitation, divorce pollution and humanism
- Nurtured in post-Christian America, in the midst of headlines about fallen televangelists and crooked politicians, lacking even the memory of a hope-giving gospel

General Characteristics

- A pervasive philosophy of moral relativity
- Very pragmatic; often not risk takers
- Pessimistic about the future
- View older adults as neither virtuous nor competent
- Express high interest in relevant spiritual issues but often look outside the Church for help
- Focused on community, survival and adaptation to change
- Have less respect for the chain of command or authority
- Not driven by long-term career goals or loyalty toward employer
- Have ambitions that are personal

Relationships and Family

- Fear long-term commitment—have delayed marriage longer than any generation since the Great Depression of the 1930s
- Key issues: *community* and the development of *deep relationships*
- Often the children of divorced, dysfunctional homes with absentee parents
- Seek a stable marriage and family
- View working motherhood as a necessity
- Unusually high suicide rates

Church

- Low trust in church authority figures and high cynicism of organized institutions
- Have left institutional churches but are searching for faith and meaning

Key Concerns

Authenticity
- Prefer honest failure rather than false successes

Community
- Want the home they never had
- Need to see the gospel lived out
- Appreciate older church members who can be an example before them

Lack of Dogmatism
- Need opportunities to work through the process of arriving at a workable value system without being chastised
- Respond to guidance that is not rigid or self-righteous

Arts
- Influenced powerfully by music and television

Diversity
- Appreciate attempts at racial reconciliation

Significance
- Crying for meaning in a world without hope

Practical Help
- Want help finding a job, locating housing, meeting friends, being a better spouse and parent

Teams
- Become committed to plans they help create
- Need to see value in what they are trying to accomplish

Methods
- Respond to discussions, storytelling and personal illustrations that allow for vulnerability

---

* For more information on Busters, see George Barna, *Boiling Point: It Only Takes One Degree* (Ventura, CA: Regal Books, 2001); also see Barna Research Group website, http://www.barna.org.

Getting to Know Boomers*
(People Born Between 1946-1963)

Important Facts

- 72.1 million born in this generation
- Raised in stable families
- Shaped by significant social and political changes of the 60s and 70s, including the shift to a consumer culture and the impact of the music and media industries
- Grew up during the Information Age, a booming economy, Free Love, war on poverty, the Vietnam war, *Happy Days* and a world gripped by humanism
- Raised during a time when science was more important than religion
- Raised in the midst of conflict: biblical, political, military and social

General Characteristics

- From hippie to yuppie to midlife righteous puritan
- Committed to things they believe have value but want to know the benefits before they commit
- Idealistic and cause oriented with the ultimate cause being themselves
- Many still searching for spiritual meaning and fulfillment in life
- Tend to be more conservative and evangelical
- Discontent with status quo
- Lean toward change based on their personal perception of the need and their own agenda
- Vain—appearance is important
- Concerned with declining health
- Workaholics with primary focus on innovation and achievement
- Built businesses around a pyramid structure and control
- Key issue: personal identity
- Focus on scientific thinking and a commonsense philosophy
- Generally raised with clear boundaries, which were challenged

Relationships and Family

- Desire to establish and maintain relationships that result in meaningful community
- Previously viewed people as a means to an end
- Older Boomers beginning to place more emphasis on meaningful relationships, especially within the family

Church

· Dropped out of church at young age; came back due to children and personal and/or business crises
· Called believers but not belongers
· Left the Church but not religion—immersed themselves in various spiritual movements, substituting many gods for the God of the Judeo-Christian faith
· Most likely adults today to be actual Christians

Key Concerns

Authenticity
· Tired of perceived dishonesty; want authenticity from church leaders, particularly from the pastor and staff

Real Answers to Real Problems
· Hard life experience; broken relationships, alcoholism, lost jobs
· Looking for a safe place

Community
· Want meaningful relationships and community

Balance Between Dogma and Need-Oriented Teaching
· Looking for a place to have their needs met
· Yearn for a simpler life
· Desire relationship with God and Christian education of their children
· Want a clear sense of purpose for living
· Need opportunity for significance

---

* For more information on Boomers, see George Barna, *Boiling Point: It Only Takes One Degree* (Ventura, CA: Regal Books, 2001); also see Barna Research Group website, http://www.barna.org.

Getting to Know Builders*
(People Born Between 1927-1945)

Important Facts

- 39.8 million born in this generation
- Raised during Industrial Revolution
- Shaped by World War I, World War II and the Great Depression
- Raised by parents for whom divorce was generally unthinkable
- Grew up with job security, unions, seniority and incomes that doubled
- Nurtured in the midst of clearly defined boundaries and a strong belief in the value of institutions

General Characteristics

- Key issues: safety, security and stability
- Believe in the importance of hard work, savings accounts and sacrificing for the good of the whole
- Feel there is safety in numbers (join clubs, etc.)
- Conservative in attitudes and actions
- Struggle with complexities of life and technological advances more than Busters
- Typically more interested in doing what honors the past than what will work
- Accept the chain-of-command authority; compliant employees
- Raised with clear boundaries but embrace relativism

Relationships and Family

- Desire meaningful relationships
- Key parenting goal: give their children a better life than they had
- Characterized by high divorce and high abortion rates
- Women restless at home during young adulthood

Church

- Of those 50 to 65 years of age, 65 percent attend weekly church services

Key Concerns

Real Help with Real Problems
- Have health concerns
- Communication issues with adult children and other complex family relationships
- Planning for retirement

Community
- Seek meaningful relationships
- Desire relationship with God
- Want sense of purpose

Opportunity for Significance
- Have stable marriages; desire to mentor younger couples

---

* For more information on Builders, see George Barna, *Boiling Point: It Only Takes One Degree* (Ventura, CA: Regal Books, 2001); also see Barna Research Group website, http://www.barna.org.

Effective Teaching Methods

Discussion

- **Agree/Disagree**—A series of controversial statements are listed, all relating to a common subject. Group members indicate whether they agree or disagree with the statements and expand on their opinion by explaining why they chose the answer they chose.
- **Brainstorming**—Group members toss around ideas regarding a common topic or question. Evaluation is withheld until all ideas are presented.
- **Buzz Groups**—Small groups of four to eight discuss a given topic for a limited period of time.
- **Case Studies**—Real-life problem situations are presented and then group members analyze the problems and suggest solutions.
- **Interviews**—Group members ask specific questions of a resource person.
- **Listening Teams**—Several small groups, each given specific questions to answer, listen to a presentation and then express their answers to the large group.
- **Word Association**—Group members are asked to share the first thoughts that come to mind at the mention of keywords.
- **Problem Solving**—A problem relating to the session theme is presented to group members, who will work together to come up with a solution.

Writing

- **Abridged Edition**—Group members read a section of Scripture and then condense it in written form to its basic meaning.
- **Group Writing**—A small group works together to complete a story, script, report or the like.
- **Lists**—Group members itemize specific ideas on worksheets or paper.
- **Open-Ended Stories**—Small groups are given unfinished stories and asked to complete them in order to resolve the story situation on the basis of scriptural principles.
- **Outlines**—Group members list the main points of an assigned Scripture passage in outline form.
- **Parables and Parallel Stories**—Group members write a contemporary story or parable to parallel a scriptural event or truth.
- **Personalized Verses**—Group members rewrite key verses using their own names and/or personal pronouns.
- **Prayer**—Group members learn to verbalize their communication with God more concretely by writing out their prayers.

Drama

- **Dramatic Readings**—Group members are assigned different parts of a Scripture narrative or prepared script and read their parts dramatically.
- **Skits**—Group members plan and/or act out a situation relating to the theme of the session.
- **Role-Play**—Group members are given specific problem situations to act out impromptu.
- **This Is Your Life**—Group members review the life of a biblical character by presenting reports from interviews of imaginary people who knew the character.

Other Methods

- **Demonstrations**—Individuals demonstrate specific tasks or skills; observers practice what has been demonstrated.
- **Research**—Group members participate in personal or group studies using the Bible, commentaries, a concordance, a dictionary, encyclopedias and the like. (This can be done during a session or assigned as homework.)
- **Seminars**—Group members attend meetings led by experts in a particular field.
- **Visual Aids**—Leaders involve the sense of sight in the teaching and learning process using chalkboards, flipcharts, overhead projectors, videotapes, charts, maps, diagrams, worksheets, demonstrations, computer presentations and the like.
- **Workshop**—Group members meet together outside the regular session to explore one or more aspects of a common interest.[1]

Note

1. Bobbie Reed, *Creative Bible Learning for Adults* (Ventura, CA: Regal Books, 1977), pp. 121-125.

Effective Discussion Techniques

When properly related to the lesson objective, discussion can be one of the finest methods for teaching adults. Discussions allow for exploration, sharing and discovery of meaning or answers. Unlike listening to a presentation or reading assignments, guided discussion emphasizes learner initiative, reflective thinking and creative expression.

The art of good discussion is tied directly to the art of asking good questions. Good questions should be pertinent and complex enough so that they cannot be answered by a simple yes or no. Beginning a question with "What about" or "How about" encourages group members to get involved. Good questions will do the following:

- Provoke thought
- Trigger remembering
- Cause people to wrestle with possible answers to problems
- Move adults beyond mere facts to a new understanding as they reason, solve problems and make judgments
- Help adults relate Scripture to contemporary problems

Types of Questions

- **Information Seeking**—This is done to obtain additional facts or more details. (For example: "What were some of the miracles that Jesus performed and what were the characteristics of those miracles?")
- **Clarifying**—This is done by asking a group member to repeat his or her answer in a different way in order to clarify what he or she meant. (For example: "Are you saying that . . . ?" or "Do you mean that . . . ?")
- **Summary or Reflective**—This may be used when you want to briefly summarize or expand what has just been said. (For example: "If I understand what we have been saying . . . Is that what we mean?")

Helpful Hints

- **Plan Ahead.** Questions should be planned and written down before you meet with your group. This assures you of better communication and avoids time-wasting clarifications.
- **Know the Response You Want.** Do you want opinions or do you want a correct answer? If you ask an opinion question (e.g., "How would you describe an ideal spouse?"), you must accept *all* answers. On the other hand, if you ask a fact question, (e.g., "What characteristics does 1 Peter 3:1-12 say an ideal wife has?"), you are looking for the *correct* answer.
- **Avoid Yes-or-No Questions.** Instead of asking "Should Christians love the world?" ask questions that invite thoughtful expression. (For example: "What does it do to a Christian when he or she loves the world?")

- **Don't Box People In.** Instead of asking, "Why is Moses a person we would want to be like?" and assume group members admire Moses, ask, "What are some qualities in Moses that a Christian might want to emulate?"

- **Have a Strategy.** There are three stages of questions to use in Bible study:

  ▸ **Stage One: Knowledge**—Questions for *recalling and stating* of facts. (For example: "What does this verse say?")
  ▸ **Stage Two: Comprehension**—Questions for *explaining* the facts. (For example: "What does this verse mean?")
  ▸ **Stage Three: Application**—Questions for *internalizing* the facts. (For example: "What does this verse mean in your life?")

  The questions in these three stages are building blocks; each is essential to the next. A person who does not know the facts cannot understand the meaning. A person who does not understand the meaning cannot explain how to apply it to life.

- **Allow Time for Group Members to Think About Their Answers.** Remember that group members are hearing your questions for the first time and need time to process the questions to come up with answers.
- **Be Aware of Spin-Off Questions.** Often, your group members will come up with answers to a question that introduce another area you would like to explore. Be ready to construct questions on the spot to cover these new thoughts. However, you will want to be sure that the spin-off discussion is not only interesting but is also of relevance to the objectives for the session. (If the new area is not relevant to the topic at hand, write down the idea for discussion later when it is more relevant to the scheduled topic.)
- **Use Clarifying Questions Liberally.** A clarifying question invites group members to expand on a discussion. Questions such as "What do you mean?" "Can you give us some examples?" and "What else can you tell us?" draw out more information and can help the group evaluate and increase its understanding of the subject.
- **Ask Questions That Lead to Positive or Constructive Answers.** Ask questions that help people decide what they can do now. Emphasize the positive things that people can do or say and play down the negative.[1]

Note

1. Bobbie Reed, *Creative Bible Learning for Adults* (Ventura, CA: Regal Books, 1977), pp. 127-153.

More Help for Leading Discussions

Be Prepared

- Make an outline or guide for the discussion (introductions, reactions, specific questions).
- List questions to stimulate thinking and discussion (unless prepared by a speaker).
- Select the proper room for your group and arrange the chairs in a semicircle, if possible.

Dos and Don'ts

Do the following:

- Allow group members to express themselves.
- Keep discussions on track for the subject at hand.
- Limit long speeches to short statements.
- Gently draw out members who are reluctant to speak up.
- Present points in a way that is understandable to all group members.
- Turn questions asked of you as the leader back to the group for discussion.
- Restate questions when discussion wavers.
- Summarize the conclusions (if any) of the group and of each group topic.
- Permit periods of silence while group members ponder their thoughts.
- Always use tact and stay alert.
- Work for an atmosphere of freedom and honesty in which all viewpoints and comments can be aired without fear of reprisal (in other words, affirm your group members!).

Avoid the following:

- Monopolizing discussions
- Allowing any one group member to dominate the discussion
- Acting as if you have all the answers
- Getting nervous when there is silence
- Answering a question before the group does
- Allowing the discussion to veer off on irrelevant subjects
- Allowing quarreling within the group
- Allowing wrong conclusions to go unquestioned
- Pretending to agree when you do not
- Hiding your own convictions
- Giving the impression that the group must always agree with you[1]

Note

1.   Bobbie Reed, *Creative Bible Learning for Adults* (Ventura, CA: Regal Books, 1977), pp. 127-153.

Lesson Planning Sheet

Class_____ Date_____

Leader_____ Coleader_____

Specific Session Aim

Methods to Utilize

Teaching Aids Needed

Session Outline

1. Approach—Stir interest.

2. Explore—Gather facts.

3. Discover—Guide understanding.

4. Apply—Lead students to ask themselves, *What does this mean to me?*

5. Assume Responsibility—Lead students to ask themselves, *What am I going to do about it?*

Personal After-Session Evaluation

1. Was my teaching aim accomplished?

2. Did my questions stimulate discussion?

3. Were group members actively involved in learning?

4. Was my teaching flexible and sensitive to the needs of the group?

5. What can I do differently next week to improve my teaching?

chapter thirteen

REPRODUCIBLE FORMS

Prayer Request Form

Name _____ Session Number _____

Phone _____ E-Mail _____

> *Now it is required that those who have been given a trust must prove faithful.*
> 1 Corinthians 4:2

Prayer Request

Remember: Prayer requests are confidential!

Prayer Request Form

Name _____ Session Number _____

Phone _____ E-Mail _____

> *Now it is required that those who have been given a trust must prove faithful.*
> 1 Corinthians 4:2

Prayer Request

Remember: Prayer requests are confidential!

Session Evaluation *(For Leaders)*

Leader _____ Coleader _____

Date_____ Attendance_____

Week_____ Topics_____

What were the most significant events in the meeting?

What weaknesses or problems did you see in the meeting?

What did you learn that you did not know before?

What follow-up is needed (e.g., a note of encouragement, a miss-you note, a phone call)?

Study Evaluation

Leader_____ Coleader_____

Study Title_____

1. Please select the statement that best describes your marriage today.

    ☐ My marriage has improved overall throughout the course of this study.
    ☐ My marriage was stable and satisfying to begin with and has stayed the same throughout this study.
    ☐ My marriage was a little shaky at the beginning of this study and has basically stayed the same.
    ☐ My marriage has declined in spite of our participation in this study.

    If you checked either of the last two boxes, would you be willing to speak with a counselor from our church so that we may offer additional help or support?   ☐ Yes   ☐ No

2. If you have experienced improvement in your marriage, please share the particular areas this study helped improve in your relationship.

3. Has this study changed your relationship with God? If so, how?

4. Was there anything you didn't like about this study or the way in which it was presented? If so, please explain.

5. Our desire is to reach marriages for Christ. How might we improve in order to better achieve this goal in the future?

6. Additional comments or suggestions.

Thank you for your honest evaluation of this study. May God continue to strengthen your relationship with Him and your relationship with your spouse.

Registration Form for Married Couples

☐ Newlywed (married fewer than 5 years)

☐ Long-term marriage (married 5 years or longer)

Meeting Day_____ Meeting Time_____

Study Title_____

Leader_____ Coleader _____

Name_____

Address _____

City_____ Zip_____

Contact Numbers

    Home_____ Other (cell, etc.)_____

    Husband's Work_____

        May we call you at work?   ☐ Yes   ☐ No

    Wife's Work_____

        May we call you at work?   ☐ Yes   ☐ No

Are you a regular attendee of this church?   ☐ Yes   ☐ No

Are you a regular attendee of another church?   ☐ Yes   ☐ No

    If so, where? _____

Would you like to receive more information about this church? ☐ Yes   ☐ No

Are you interested in child care?   ☐ Yes   ☐ No

    If yes, please list name(s) and age(s) of child(ren) to be placed.

_____ *DO NOT WRITE BELOW THIS LINE* _____

Paid   ☐ Yes   ☐ No

Amount $_____Check #_____or ☐ Cash

Class Assignment: Day _____ Time_____ Leader_____

Materials Received   ☐ Yes   ☐ No

Registration Form for Engaged Couples

Meeting Day_____ Meeting Time_____

Study Title_____

Leader_____ Coleader _____

For Her

Name_____

Address _____

City_____ Zip_____

Contact Numbers

    Home_____ Other (cell, etc.)_____

    Work_____

        May we call you at work?   ☐ Yes   ☐ No

Are you a regular attendee of this church?   ☐ Yes   ☐ No

Are you a regular attendee of another church?

    If so, where? _____

Would you like to receive more information about this church? ☐ Yes   ☐ No

For Him

Name_____

Address _____

City_____ Zip_____

Contact Numbers

    Home_____ Other (cell, etc.)_____

    Work_____

        May we call you at work?   ☐ Yes   ☐ No

Are you a regular attendee of this church?   ☐ Yes   ☐ No

Are you a regular attendee of another church?   ☐ Yes   ☐ No

    If so, where? _____

Would you like to receive more information about this church? ☐ Yes   ☐ No

_____ *DO NOT WRITE BELOW THIS LINE* _____

Paid   ☐ Yes   ☐ No

Amount $_____ Check #_____or ☐ Cash

Class Assignment: Day _____ Time_____ Leader_____

Materials Received   ☐ Yes   ☐ No

Getting to Know the Bride

Tell Us About You!

Full Name (first, middle and last)_____

Birth Date_____ Age_____

Street Address_____

City_____ State_____ Zip_____

Home Phone _____ Other (cell, etc.)_____

Employer_____ Position_____

Work Phone_____

Are you a member of this church? ☐ Yes ☐ No

    If no, where is your home church?_____

Tell Us About Your Parents

Father's Name_____

Home Phone_____ Other (cell, etc.)_____

Is your father a member of this church? ☐ Yes ☐ No

    If no, where is his home church?_____

Mother's Name_____

Home Phone_____ Other (cell, etc.)_____

Is your mother a member of this church? ☐ Yes ☐ No

    If no, where is her home church?_____

Getting to Know the Groom

Tell Us About You!

Full Name (first, middle and last)_____

Birth Date_____. Age_____

Street Address_____

City_____ State_____ Zip_____

Home Phone _____ Other (cell, etc.)_____

Employer_____ Position_____

Work Phone_____

Are you a member of this church?   ☐ Yes   ☐ No

　　If no, where is your home church?_____

Tell Us About Your Parents

Father's Name_____

Home Phone_____ Other (cell, etc.)_____

Is your father a member of this church?   ☐ Yes   ☐ No

　　If no, where is his home church?_____

Mother's Name_____

Home Phone_____ Other (cell, etc.)_____

Is your mother a member of this church?   ☐ Yes   ☐ No

　　If no, where is her home church?_____

Getting to Know the Couple

Note: Wedding and rehearsal dates and times will be discussed in detail when you meet with the minister.

About Your Ceremony

Requested Wedding Date_____

Requested Time of Day_____ A.M. / P.M._____

About Your Rehearsal

Requested Rehearsal Date_____

Requested Time of Day_____ A.M. / P.M._____

Requested Location for Rehearsal_____

Requested Minister (from this church)_____

Second Minister (from another church)_____

    Affiliation _____ Phone_____

About Your Preparation Thus Far

1. What books or other materials on marriage have you read in the past two years?

   Bride

   Groom

2. Are your parents supportive of your marriage plans?
   Bride   ☐ Yes   ☐ No
   Groom   ☐ Yes   ☐ No

3. If you are not a member or regular attendee of this church, tell us why you are requesting to have your wedding ceremony here.

4. What are two or three areas you hope will be covered in your marriage-preparation classes?

   Bride

   Groom

5. Have you ever been married before?

   Bride   ☐ Yes   ☐ No

   Groom   ☐ Yes   ☐ No

   If so, what ended the marriage?

   Bride   ☐ Death of Spouse   ☐ Divorce

   Groom   ☐ Death of Spouse   ☐ Divorce

6. Who will be the primary contact for wedding details? (If someone other than the bride, groom or either parents, please provide name and contact information.)

Planning the Order of Service Worksheet

Wedding of (bride)_____ and (groom)_____

Wedding Date_____ Time_____A.M. / P.M.

Sanctuary_____.

If Your Wedding Is Scheduled on a Saturday
Do you want to leave your wedding flowers for Sunday morning? ☐ Yes ☐ No

Ceremony Participants

Minister(s):

Soloist(s):

Vocalist(s):

Additional Instrumentalists:

Other Participants:

Selecting the Elements of Your Ceremony

The following is a sample of what may be included in an order of service. Place a check mark next to the elements you would like to include in your ceremony. (You'll decide the order in the next section.)

____ Prelude music (15 to 30 minutes)   ____ Exchange of vows

____ Seating of the family   ____ Exchange of rings

____ Solo   ____ Prayer for the bride and groom

____ Processional   ____ Solo

____ Bride's processional   ____ Lighting of the unity candle

____ Call to worship   ____ Pronouncement of marriage

____ Opening prayer   ____ Benediction

____ Questions of intent   ____ Recessional

____ Relinquishment of the bride   ____ Postlude

____ Scripture reading(s)

____ Wedding meditation, homily or
     charge to the bride and groom

Selecting Your Order of Service

Now that you have selected your preferred elements for your ceremony, list them below in the order you want them to occur. Add any elements that were not included in the previous list but that you would like to have in your ceremony.

Prospective Mentor-Couple Questionnaire*

Husband's Name_____

Wife's Name_____

Street Address_____

City_____ Zip_____

Home Phone_____ Work Phone_____

E-Mail _____

Thank you for your interest in becoming a lay-ministry mentor couple in our church's marriage ministry and within this community. Since this ministry is so important to our church, its marriages and its families and because many aspects of the ministry can be sensitive, it is important that the selection committee learn a little about you and your marriage. Therefore, you are requested to please prayerfully and thoughtfully complete this questionnaire as part of your application process. All information furnished will be held in strict confidence by members of the selection committee.

1. How long have you been members or adherents at our church?

2. How long have each of you been a Christian?
   Husband
   Wife

3. What was your wedding date (month, day, year)?

4. Is this your first (or original) marriage? If no, please explain.

5. Do you have children? If yes, what are their ages?

6. Place a check mark next to your temperament.

   Husband
   ☐ Sanguine   ☐ Choleric   ☐ Melancholic   ☐ Phlegmatic

   Wife
   ☐ Sanguine   ☐ Choleric   ☐ Melancholic   ☐ Phlegmatic

7. What is your primary love language?

Husband

Wife

8. Please explain why you, as a couple, would like to become a part of this church's marriage ministry?

9. Please describe any prior marriage ministry experience you may have had. Prior experience is not a prerequisite to participation in our marriage ministry program.

10. What about your marriage (and/or you as a couple) do you feel would make you effective as a mentor couple in this marriage ministry? How might you help other couples who are struggling in their marriage?

11. Briefly describe when you accepted Christ as Lord and Savior (i.e., the date and/or event) and your growth as a Christian.

Husband

Wife

12. Briefly describe your biblical understanding of the role and importance of marriage in the Church, in the family and in society.

13. Are you comfortable sharing as a couple about the strengths and weaknesses of your marriage—both historic and present—in order to help other married couples who are experiencing struggles?

☐ Yes   ☐ No   ☐ Not entirely

Please explain any limitations or hesitations you feel about this type of sharing.

14. The areas of potential involvement for married couples in this church's marriage ministry include the following. Please check those for which you would like to be considered.

☐ Mentor couple to meet regularly over several months with engaged couples—one couple at a time—that are preparing for marriage.

☐ Mentor couple to meet over several months with newly married couples—one couple at a time—that are having beginning marriage challenges and have asked for the counsel of a more experienced married couple.

☐ Mentor couple to work specifically with couples in second and/or blended family marriages that have requested help.

☐ Mentor couple to work over several months with married couples in significant crises—one couple at a time—but who have not given up hope and are not yet to the point of needing or desiring professional marriage counseling.

☐ Couple to help with pre-, during, or postseminar logistical support for our marriage-enrichment seminars, engaged-encounter weekends or couples retreats.

15. Do you have any reservations and/or questions about this church's marriage ministry that you would like to discuss before you decide whether or not you wish to formally pursue approval for involvement in this ministry?

16. A married couple's work with a couple seeking help from this church's marriage ministry may be extremely sensitive and always must be handled with utmost confidentiality. Would each of you, individually and as a couple, be fully comfortable with these characteristics and requirements of the ministry?

Husband ☐ Yes ☐ No
Wife ☐ Yes ☐ No

Husband's Signature _____ Date _____

Wife's Signature _____ Date _____

* Dick and Carol Cronk, and Kent and Mary Dyer, *Growth in Marriage* (Dayton, OH: Christian Life Center, 2002). Call 1-877-272-8585 for more information about the Marriage Builders Ministry.

PUBLICITY AIDS

Let's face it: The more people who hear or read about your marriage ministry, the more people you will attract. This includes those who will help in the ministry and those who will benefit from it.

If publicity is not your area of expertise, take the time to find someone who has publicity experience or ability. Publicity is vital to reaching, not only those in your church, but also those who don't even know your church exists. Publicity is a great method for drawing newcomers to your church. Why? Because people in the church aren't the only ones who care about developing strong marriages—people in the world do, too! Publicize your ministry in the local community as a way to help them in their endeavor to do just that.

Church Publicity Ideas

Use Printed Information
- Bulletin inserts
- Articles in the church newsletter
- Posters placed inside the church building at various locations
- Brochures
- Letters

Use Verbal Presentations
- Announcements in classes and from the pulpit
- Dramatic presentations
- Interviews with graduates
- Success stories given in person or videotaped

Community Publicity Ideas

Advertise Your Marital Preparation Ministry
- Buy ads or write articles to be placed in local bridal magazines, college newspapers, community newspapers, etc.
- Display business cards or brochures at bridal shops and store gift registry desks.
- Ask the publisher of your local yellow pages to see if the publisher will donate ad space to publicize church and community marriage-strengthening events.

Advertise Marriage Enrichment and Intervention Classes and Mentoring

- Record radio ads.
- Leave business cards and brochures (with permission) in counseling offices, health clubs, family-law attorney offices, etc.
- Place posters and flyers (with permission) on domestic-court bulletin boards.
- Work with officials at your local courthouse.

Advertise Other Aspects of Your Marriage Ministry

- Set up displays and distribute literature at community events.
- Encourage ministry workers to invite friends to participate.
- Advertise on your church's marquee.
- Purchase advertising (or get local businesses to sponsor advertising) on billboards or park benches.
- Place posters, brochures and business cards (with permission) on the bulletin boards of apartment complexes.
- Cooperate with the schools in your neighborhood (e.g., perhaps the school would let you put flyers in with their parent information).
- Cooperate with the family-court system.

Is Your Marriage Sinking in Quicksand?

Rebuild Your Foundation on Solid Rock.

Focus on the Family's Marriage Series Presents

The Covenant Marriage

Orientation Meeting
Sunday, January 26th, 7:00 P.M. – 8:30 P.M.

After-Dinner Refreshments! · Free Child Care! · Giveaways!

. . . .

Come for the Freebies—Stay for the Hope.

My City Community Church, 123 Anytown Lane.
For more information, please call the church office at (555) 555-5555.

It's Coming! Don't Miss It!

Focus on the Family Marriage Series

Are you engaged? Newlywed? Been married for years and have
a desire to have a marriage as God designed it?
Well, look no further! We are proud to present

The Masterpiece Marriage

This four-week study will help you develop the tools you need to
build a marriage that's everything you've ever dreamed and more.
With God as the center of your relationship, you'll learn
how putting Christ first in your life will have a profound
impact on your relationship with your spouse.

Wednesdays from 7:00 P.M. to 8:30 P.M. starting in mid-February

More Details Coming Soon!

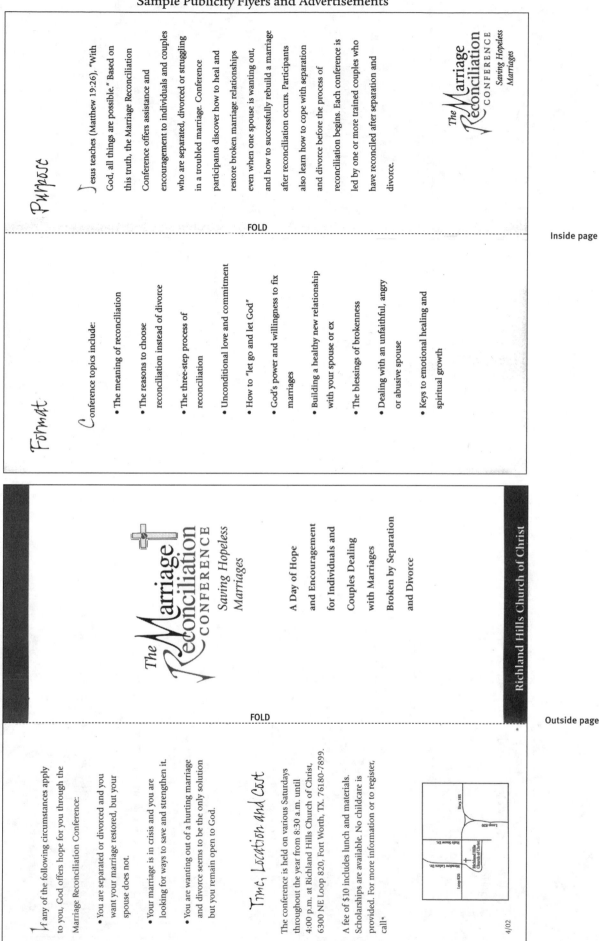

Inside page

Purpose

Jesus teaches (Matthew 19:26), "With God, all things are possible." Based on this truth, the Marriage Reconciliation Conference offers assistance and encouragement to individuals and couples who are separated, divorced or struggling in a troubled marriage. Conference participants discover how to heal and restore broken marriage relationships even when one spouse is wanting out, and how to successfully rebuild a marriage after reconciliation occurs. Participants also learn how to cope with separation and divorce before the process of reconciliation begins. Each conference is led by one or more trained couples who have reconciled after separation and divorce.

The **Marriage Reconciliation** CONFERENCE
Saving Hopeless Marriages

Format

Conference topics include:

- The meaning of reconciliation
- The reasons to choose reconciliation instead of divorce
- The three-step process of reconciliation
- Unconditional love and commitment
- How to "let go and let God"
- God's power and willingness to fix marriages
- Building a healthy new relationship with your spouse or ex
- The blessings of brokenness
- Dealing with an unfaithful, angry or abusive spouse
- Keys to emotional healing and spiritual growth

Outside page

The **Marriage Reconciliation** CONFERENCE
Saving Hopeless Marriages

A Day of Hope and Encouragement for Individuals and Couples Dealing with Marriages Broken by Separation and Divorce

Richland Hills Church of Christ

If any of the following circumstances apply to you, God offers hope for you through the Marriage Reconciliation Conference:

- You are separated or divorced and you want your marriage restored, but your spouse does not.
- Your marriage is in crisis and you are looking for ways to save and strengthen it.
- You are wanting out of a hurting marriage and divorce seems to be the only solution but you remain open to God.

Time, Location and Cost

The conference is held on various Saturdays throughout the year from 8:30 a.m. until 4:00 p.m. at Richland Hills Church of Christ, 6300 NE Loop 820, Fort Worth, TX. 76180-7899.

A fee of $10 includes lunch and materials. Scholarships are available. No childcare is provided. For more information or to register, call*

4/02

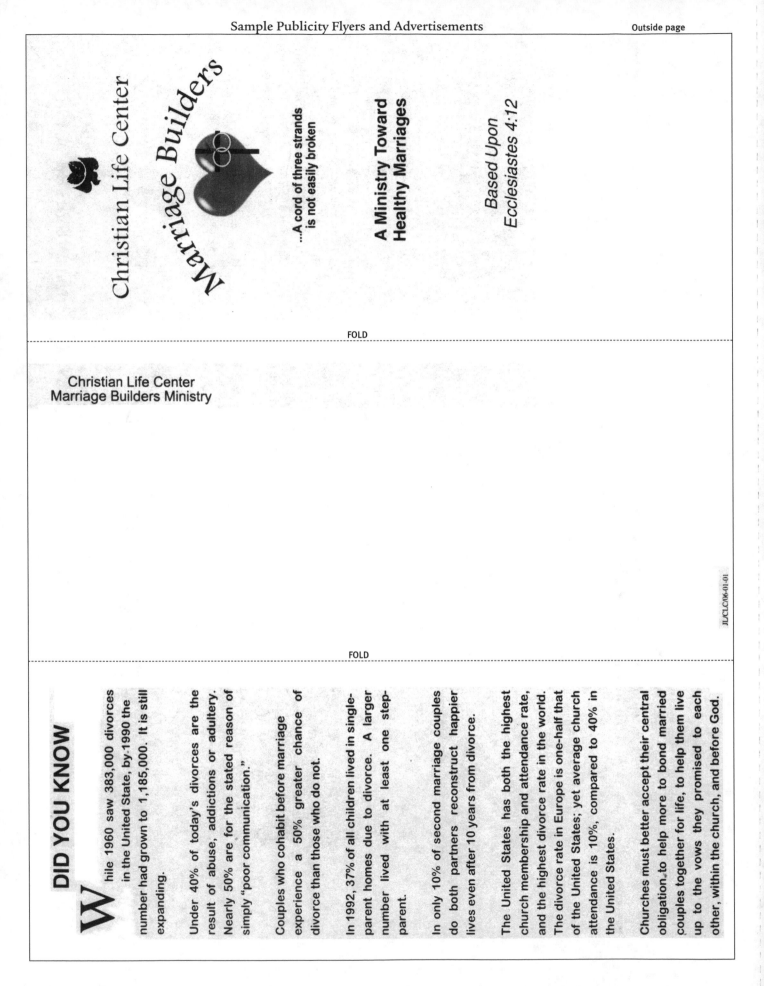

Christian Life Center

Marriage Builders

...A cord of three strands
is not easily broken

A Ministry Toward
Healthy Marriages

Based Upon
Ecclesiastes 4:12

FOLD

Christian Life Center
Marriage Builders Ministry

JLCLC\06-01-01

FOLD

DID YOU KNOW

While 1960 saw 383,000 divorces in the United State, by 1990 the number had grown to 1,185,000. It is still expanding.

Under 40% of today's divorces are the result of abuse, addictions or adultery. Nearly 50% are for the stated reason of simply "poor communication."

Couples who cohabit before marriage experience a 50% greater chance of divorce than those who do not.

In 1992, 37% of all children lived in single-parent homes due to divorce. A larger number lived with at least one step-parent.

In only 10% of second marriage couples do both partners reconstruct happier lives even after 10 years from divorce.

The United States has both the highest church membership and attendance rate, and the highest divorce rate in the world. The divorce rate in Europe is one-half that of the United States; yet average church attendance is 10%, compared to 40% in the United States.

Churches must better accept their central obligation...to help more to bond married couples together for life, to help them live up to the vows they promised to each other, within the church, and before God.

MARRIAGE ASSISTANCE

The focus of the Marriage Assistance division of CLC's Marriage Builders Ministry is to help couples through periods of serious marital challenges, struggles or crises.

Methods utilized to promote healing and to re-instill growth include trained and experienced mentor couples, pastoral counseling, rediscovery weekend experiences at various locations, professional counseling referrals and other proven successful Christian based resources.

If you are a married couple who is experiencing stress in your marriage, for confidential information on how Marriage Assistance can help you, telephone the Marriage Builders Ministry at 937-667-2153.

FOLD

MARRIAGE ENRICHMENT

Toward the goal of life-long, healthy marriages, Christian Life Center conducts Marriage Enrichment seminars and retreats, plus promotes Marriage Encounter weekends, Family Life Weekends To Remember, the Fall Festival of Marriage, and other marriage enrichment experiences at various locations.

In addition, the Marriage Enrichment division promotes married couples Sunday School classes and Growth Groups. Excellent audio and video tapes and tape series, books, workbooks, and magazines on various aspects of marriage are also available through Marriage Builders.

If you are a married couple who is seeking meaningful ways to enhance your positive growth, for more information about Marriage Enrichment activities and resources, telephone the Marriage Builders Ministry of Christian Life Center at 898-8811, Ext. 227.

FOLD

MARRIAGE PREPARATION

At Christian Life Center we hold the highest view of marriage and do everything we can to help a couple prepare for their married life together.

This Marriage Preparation process, a prerequisite to be married at CLC, includes: pastoral counseling, a seasoned married mentor couple who works with the engaged couple in their premarital preparation process and during their newlywed year; conducting AG Engaged Encounter weekends at CLC; administration of the FOCCUS or PREPARE premarital inventories; and providing a Wedding Coordinator who works with the couple and family on the logistics of conducting a wedding at Christian Life Center.

If you are an engaged couple desiring to be married at Christian Life Center, call 898-8811, Ext. 34. For information about the Marriage Preparation process, telephone the Marriage Builders ministry of Christian Life Center at 890-7078.

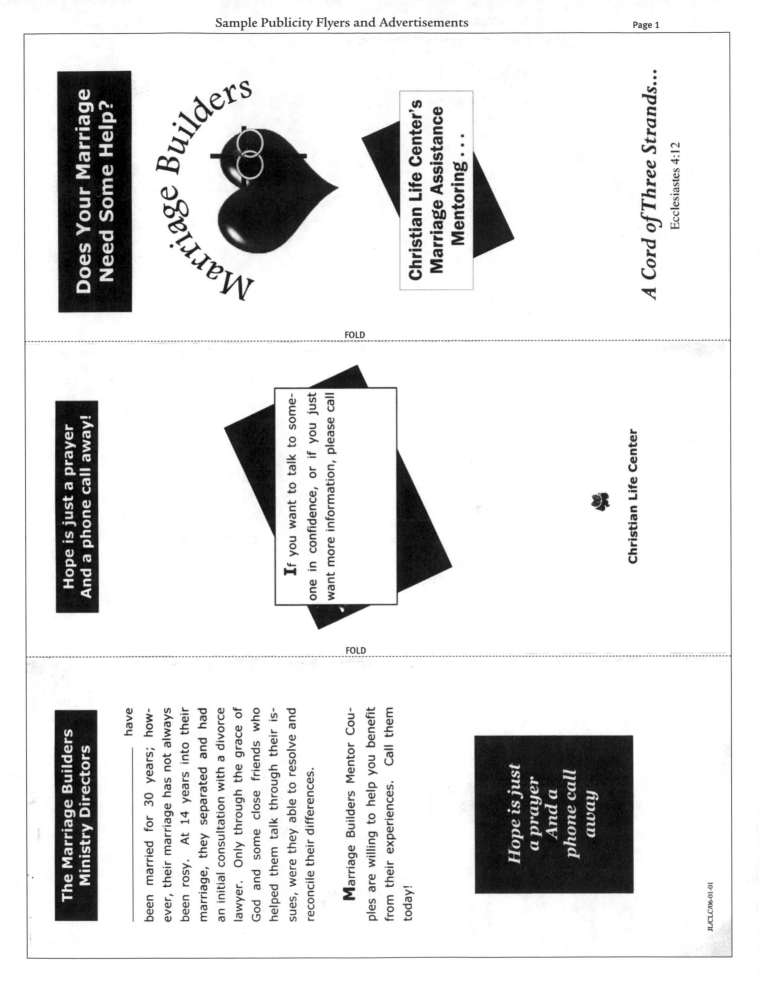

Does Your Marriage Need Some Help?

Marriage Builders

Christian Life Center's Marriage Assistance Mentoring . . .

A Cord of Three Strands...
Ecclesiastes 4:12

FOLD

Hope is just a prayer And a phone call away!

If you want to talk to someone in confidence, or if you just want more information, please call

Christian Life Center

FOLD

The Marriage Builders Ministry Directors

_____ have been married for 30 years; however, their marriage has not always been rosy. At 14 years into their marriage, they separated and had an initial consultation with a divorce lawyer. Only through the grace of God and some close friends who helped them talk through their issues, were they able to resolve and reconcile their differences.

Marriage Builders Mentor Couples are willing to help you benefit from their experiences. Call them today!

Hope is just a prayer And a phone call away

JLCLC006-01-01

Other Annual Events

- Marriage Enrichment Seminar
- Married Couples Retreat
- Engaged Encounters
- World Marriage Day Recognition
- New Mentor Couple Training

WATCH THE CLC BULLETIN FOR EVENT INFORMATION

Christian Life Center

FOLD

Marriage Mentoring

Marriage Mentoring is not professional counseling, but is meeting with a couple who has "been through the fire" in their own marriage relationship; and now has a stable marriage and is willing to share their lessons learned with you.

A series of mentoring sessions will center around your particular marriage issues and will cover:

- Marital Evaluations
- Personality Differences
- Communication
- Conflict Resolution
- Intimacy
- Growth
- Scripture & Prayer

HISTORY

Over the four years that the Marriage Builders Ministry has been in operation, over 170 couples have taken advantage of the value available through a trained and experienced mentor couple.

Marriage mentoring is strictly confidential in terms of both: (1) which married couples are involved in the program and (2) the content of mentoring sessions. A series usually lasts 14-20 weeks, meeting together typically every other week.

FOLD

The Challenges of Marriage

In the Cinderella story, the couple "lives happily ever after." However, in our society, with the pressures of conflicting demands, and too little time, marriage relationships are often taken for granted. With all the distractions, we easily forget that strong, caring, loving marriages take work.

Without attention and care, marriages wither. Couples slowly and quietly drift apart by hurtful words and actions. For many, it has been a very long time since they knew the joy of a loving relationship. Some even feel they are staying together "for the sake of the kids."

Marriage Assistance Mentors help such couples "put the pieces back together" and rebuild loving relationships.

If your marriage experiences frequent battles, or there is little or no meaningful communication, or if you are even contemplating separation or divorce, we believe the Marriage Builders Mentor Ministry may be able to help you.

Are You Planning to Get Married?

- How do I know he/she is the right person?"
- What can we learn together to help assure our successful marriage ?
- What are the procedures and requirements to marry at CLC?

Christian Life Center
Marriage Builders
Ministry

FOLD

CLC Marriage Builders Ministry

FOLD

Frequently Asked Questions

To marry at CLC, you or a family member must have been attending CLC for at least six months.

CLC has a wedding coordinator to help the couple coordinate the logistics of a wedding at CLC.

Wedding dates are not available 30 days prior to Easter and the month of December.

The Montgomery County Marriage License Bureau info line is 225-4656. Numbers for other counties available upon request.

CLC Marriage Builders Ministry conducts annual Engaged Encounter weekends, Couples Retreats, Marriage Seminars, and a weekly Marriage Sunday School Class.

Getting Married

If you are thinking about getting married at CLC, contact the Marriage Builders secretary,

AT LEAST SIX MONTHS before your planned wedding date.

This office will check your requested date for availability, help you select and schedule a meeting with a pastor to perform the ceremony, refer you to the CLC Wedding Coordinator and put you in contact with the Marriage Builders Ministry Preparation Division to start your required marriage preparation process.

FOLD

Engaged

Over a several month period of time, a married Mentor Couple will teach and coach you on interpersonal relationship skills that will help you prepare for the challenges of marriage, including:

A. A pre-marital inventory that will help you identify those areas where you share potential strengths and those where you may need growth.

B. Understanding your temperament differences.

C. Communication skills.

D. Conflict resolution skills.

E. Nurturing physical, spiritual, and emotional intimacy.

F. Developing a budget.

**Christian Life Center
Marriage Builders
Ministry
3489 Little York Road**

FOLD

Seriously Dating

Using the book "Finding the Love of Your Life—10 Principles for Choosing the Right Marriage Partner," a Marriage Builders Mentor Couple will discuss with you how to eliminate the seven most prevalent causes of faulty mate selection.

Using the video series, "How to Avoid Marrying A Jerk," you will learn:

(a) What the bonding factors are and what the dividers are in a relationship.

(b) Why time, talking and togetherness are important.

(c) Why you can't marry Jethro without getting the Clampett's.

RESOURCES

Marriage Strengthening

Engaged Couples

Hardin, Jerry. *Getting Ready for Marriage Workbook*. Nashville, TN: Thomas Nelson, 1992.

LaHaye, Tim and Beverly. *The Act of Marriage*. Rev. ed. Grand Rapids, MI: Zondervan Publishing House, 1998.

National Association of Marriage Enhancement. *Preparing for the Covenant of Marriage, Workbook Edition*.
    Order at www.nameonline.net, resource ID #PM-01.

Parrott, Les and Leslie. *Saving Your Marriage Before It Starts*. Grand Rapids, MI: Zondervan Corporation, 1995.

Phillips, Bob. *How Can I Be Sure? Questions to Ask Before You Get Married*. Eugene, OR: Harvest House, 1999.

Rainey, Dennis. *Preparing for Marriage*. Ventura, CA: Gospel Light, 1997.

——. *Preparing for Marriage Leader's Guide*. Ventura, CA: Gospel Light, 1997.

——. *Starting Your Marriage Right*. Nashville, TN: Thomas Nelson, 2000.

Rainey, Dennis and Barbara. *We Still Do: Celebrating Love for a Lifetime*. Nashville, TN: Thomas Nelson, 2001.

Warren, Neil Clark. *Finding the Love of Your Life: Ten Principles for Choosing the Right Marriage Partner*.
    Wheaton, IL: Tyndale House Publishers, 1994.

Wright, H. Norman. *Before You Say, I Do*. Rev. ed. Eugene, OR: Harvest House, 1997.

——. *So You're Getting Married*. Ventura, CA: Regal Books, 1985.

Enrichment

Books and Curricula

Alpha North America. *The Marriage Course: How to Build a Healthy Marriage That Lasts a Lifetime*. New York:
    Alpha North America, 2000.

Anderson, Neil. *The Christ-Centered Marriage*. Ventura, CA: Regal Books, 1996.

Arthur, Kay. *A Marriage Without Regrets Study Guide*. Eugene, OR: Harvest House, 2000.

Barnhill, Julie Ann. *'Till Debt Do Us Part: Answers and Healing for Money Conflicts in Your Marriage*. Eugene, OR:
    Harvest House, 2002.

Burkett, Larry. *The World's Easiest Pocket Guide to Money and Marriage*. Chicago: Northfield Publishing, 2002.

Chapman, Gary. *The Five Love Languages*. Chicago: Moody Press, 1996.

Clark, David. *A Marriage After God's Own Heart*. Sisters, OR: Multnomah Publishers, 2001.

Dobson, James. *Love Must Be Tough*. Waco, TX: Word Publishing, 1983.

———. *Love for a Lifetime*. Sisters, OR: Multnomah Publishers, 1998.

Farrel, Bill and Pam. *Men Are Like Waffles—Women Are Like Spaghetti: Understanding and Delighting in Your Differences*. Eugene, OR: Harvest House, 2001.

Group Publishing. *Improving Communication in Your Marriage*. Loveland, CO: Idea Group Publishing, 2000.

Hall, Laurie. *An Affair of the Mind*. Wheaton, IL: Tyndale House Publishers, 1996.

Harley, Willard F., Jr. *His Needs, Her Needs*. Ada, MI: Fleming H. Revell, 2001.

———. *Love Busters: Overcoming Habits That Destroy Romantic Love*. Rev. ed. Ada, MI: Baker Book House, 2002.

———. *Fall in Love, Stay in Love*. Grand Rapids, MI: Fleming H. Revell, 2001.

———. *Five Steps to Romantic Love Workbook*. Ada, MI: Fleming H. Revell, 1997. (Workbook for *Love Busters* and *His Needs, Her Needs*.)

———. *Surviving an Affair*. Ada, MI: Fleming H. Revell, 1998.

Horne, Bob and Jan. *Resolving Conflict in Your Marriage*. Loveland, CO: Idea Group Publishing, 2000.

Hybels, Bill. *Fit to Be Tied: Making Marriage Last a Lifetime*. Grand Rapids, MI: Zondervan Publishing House, 1993.

Janssen, Al. *The Marriage Masterpiece*. Grand Rapids, MI: Zondervan Publishing House, 2001.

Jenkins, Jerry. *Loving Your Marriage Enough to Protect It*. Chicago: Moody Press, 2000.

Leman, Kevin. *Becoming a Couple of Promise*. Colorado Springs, CO: NavPress, 1999.

Littauer, Florence. *Personality Plus for Couples: Understanding Yourself and the One You Love*. Ada, MI: Baker Book House, 2001.

Longman, Tremper, and Dan Allender. *Intimate Allies*. Wheaton, IL: Tyndale House Publishers, 1999.

Meredith, Don and Sally. *Two Becoming One Workbook*. Chicago: Moody Press, 1999.

Mintle, Linda. *Divorce Proofing Your Marriage*. Lake Mary, FL: Siloam Press, 2001.

Parrott, Les and Leslie. *When Bad Things Happen to Good Marriages: How to Stay Together When Life Pulls You Apart*. Grand Rapids, MI: Zondervan Publishing House, 2001.

Rainey, Dennis. *Building Your Marriage*. Loveland, CO: Group Publishing, 2000.

———. *Simply Romantic Nights*. Family Life Publishing, 2001.

Rainey, Dennis and Barbara. *Moments Together for Couples: A Daily Devotional*. Ventura, CA: Regal Books, 2003.

Rosberg, Gary. *Do-It-Yourself Relationship Mender*. Rev. ed. Wheaton, IL: Tyndale House Publishers, 1995.

Sande, Ken. *Peacemaking for Families: A Biblical Guide to Managing Conflict in Your Home*. Wheaton, IL: Tyndale House Publishers, 2002.

Smalley, Gary, and John Trent. *Love Is a Decision*. New York: Simon and Schuster, 1992.

Swindoll, Charles. *Strike the Original Match*. Wheaton, IL: Tyndale House Publishers, 1990.

Thomas, Gary. *Sacred Marriage: What If God Designed Marriage to Make Us Holy More Than to Make Us Happy?* Grand Rapids, MI: Zondervan Publishing House, 2002.

Vernick, Leslie. *How to Act Right When Your Spouse Acts Wrong*. Colorado Springs, CO: Waterbrook Press, 2001.

Waite, Linda J., and Maggie Gallagher. *The Case for Marriage: Why Married People Are Happier, Healthier and Better Off Financially*. New York: Doubleday, 2000.

Wheat, Ed, and Gloria Okes Perkins. *Love Life for Every Married Couple*. Grand Rapids, MI: Zondervan Publishing House, 1980.

———. *Staying in Love for a Lifetime*. Grand Rapids, MI: Zondervan Publishing House, 1996. (Includes *Love for Every Married Couple*, *The First Years of Forever* and *Secret Choices*.)

Wright, H. Norman. *How to Counsel a Couple in Six Sessions or Less*. Ventura, CA: Regal Books, 2002.

———. *The Marriage Checkup*. Ventura, CA: Regal Books, 2002.

———. *The Marriage Checkup Questionnaire*. Ventura, CA: Regal Books, 2002.

Audio and Video Curricula

Arp, David and Claudia. *The Second Half of Marriage: Facing the Eight Challenges of Every Long-Term Marriage.* Grand Rapids, MI: Zondervan Publishing House, 2000. A book and video curriculum series designed to help aging Boomers revitalize their marriage.

Bevere, Lisa. *Be Angry but Don't Blow It!* Nashville, TN: Thomas Nelson, 2000. (Part of the book and video series titled Healing for the Angry Heart.)

Cloud, Henry. *Changes That Heal: How to Understand Your Past to Ensure a Healthier Future.* Grand Rapids, MI: Zondervan Publishing House, 1992. (Order the book, audio and video series at www.cloudtownsend.com.)

Cloud, Henry, and John Townsend. *Boundaries.* Grand Rapids, MI: Zondervan Publishing House, 1992. (Order the book, audio and video series at www.cloudtownsend.com.)

——. *Boundaries in Marriage.* Grand Rapids, MI: Zondervan Publishing House, 1992. (Order the book, audio and video series at www.cloudtownsend.com.)

Smalley, Gary. *Hidden Keys of a Loving, Lasting Marriage.* Grand Rapids, MI: Zondervan Publishing House, 1993.

——. *Secrets to Lasting Love: Uncovering the Keys to Life-Long Intimacy.* New York: Simon and Schuster, 2002.

——. *Homes of Honor*, Relationship Series. (Order this two-part video series at http://.store.smalley.cc.)

——. *Making Love Last Forever.* Waco, TX: Word Publishing, 1998. (The leader's guide is available at http://store.smalley.cc.)

Townsend, John. *Hiding from Love: How to Change the Withdrawal Patterns That Isolate and Imprison You.* Grand Rapids, MI: Zondervan Publishing House, 1996. (Order the workbook and video kit at www.cloudtownsend.com.)

Intervention

Books

Church Initiative. *Before You Divorce.* (Order at www.beforeyoudivorce.org.)

Clinton, Timothy. *Before a Bad Goodbye.* Nashville, TN: Word Publishing, 1999.

Markman, Howard; Scott M. Stanley; and Susan L. Blumberg. *Fighting for Your Marriage: Positive Steps for Preventing Divorce and Preserving a Lasting Love.* San Francisco: Jossey-Bass, 2001.

Talley, Jim A., and Leslie Stobbe. *Reconcilable Differences.* Exp. Ed. Nashville, TN: Nelson Publishers, 1991.

Wallerstein, Judith; Julia Lewis; and Sandra Blakeslee. *The Unexpected Legacy of Divorce: A 25-Year Landmark Study.* New York: Hyperion, 2000.

Curricula

Church Initiative. *Before You Divorce.* Wake Forest, NC: Church Initiative. Includes video sessions, workbook and couple's guide. Order at www.beforeyoudivorce.org.

Williams, Joe and Michelle Williams: *Reconciling God's Way Workbook.* Includes *Support Partner Workbook.* Order at www.reconcilinggodsway.com.

Divorce Recovery/Remarriage

Dunn, Dick. *Preparing to Marry Again.* Nashville, TN: Discipleship Resources, 1999. (Order at www.marriagesavers.com.)

Keller, Jim. *Making Your Remarriage Last.* Loveland, CO: Group Publishing, 2001.

Wright, H. Norman. *Before You Remarry.* Rev. ed. Eugene, OR: Harvest House, 1999.

Blended Families

Dunn, Dick. *Willing to Try Again—Steps Toward Blending a Family.* Valley Forge, PA: Judson Press, 1993.
———. *Developing a Successful Stepfamily Ministry.* (Order at www.marriagesavers.com.)

Individual Strengthening

Basic Discipleship

Barna, George. *Growing True Disciples.* Ventura, CA: Issachar Resources, 2000.

Blackaby, Henry T., and Claude V King. *Experiencing God.* Nashville, TN: LifeWay Press, 1998.

Guinness, Os, comp. *When No One Sees: The Importance of Character in an Age of Image.* Colorado Springs: CO: NavPress, 2000.

Hunt, T. W. *The Mind of Christ: The Transforming Power of Thinking His Thoughts.* Nashville, TN: Broadman and Holman, 1995.

Moore, Beth. *Breaking Free: Making Liberty with Christ a Reality in Life.* Nashville, TN: LifeWay Press, 1999.

The Navigators. *Deepening Your Roots in God's Family: A Course in Personal Discipleship to Strengthen Your Walk with God.* Colorado Springs, CO: Navpress, 1999.

———. Design for Discipleship Series. Rev. ed. Colorado Springs, CO: NavPress, 1990.

———. *Growing Strong in God's Family: A Course in Personal Discipleship to Strengthen Your Walk with God.* Colorado Springs, CO: NavPress, 1999.

Ogden, Greg. *Discipleship Essentials: A Guide to Rebuilding Your Life in Christ.* Westmont, IL: InterVarsity Press, 1998.

Smith, Michael M. *Nurturing a Passion for Prayer: A Discipleship Journal Bible Study on Prayer.* Colorado Springs, CO: NavPress, 2000.

Men

Arterburn, Stephen. *Every Man's Battle: Winning the War on Sexual Temptation One Battle at a Time.* Colorado Springs, CO: WaterBrook Press, 2000.

Dobson, James. *What Wives Wish Their Husbands Knew About Women.* Wheaton, IL: Tyndale House, 1975.

Donovan, Daryl G. *Men Mentoring Men: A Men's Discipleship Course.* Lima, OH: C. S. S. Publishing Company, 1998.

Donovan, Daryl G. and Bill McCartney. *Men Mentoring Men Again: Men's Discipleship Course.* Lima, OH: C. S. S. Publishing Company, 2000.

Lepine, Bob. *The Christian Husband: God's Vision for Loving and Caring for Your Wife.* Ann Arbor, MI: Vine Books, 1999.

Omartian, Stormie. *The Power of a Praying Husband.* Eugene, OR: Harvest House, 2001.

Peel, William Carr. *What God Does When Men Pray: A Small Group Discussion Guide.* Colorado Springs, CO: NavPress, 1993.

Rainey, Dennis. *Two Hearts Are Better Than One: A Journal for Husbands.* Nashville, TN: Thomas Nelson, 1999.

Scott, Stuart. *The Exemplary Husband: A Biblical Perspective.* Bemidji, MN: Focus Publishing, 2000.

Smalley, Gary. *Winning Your Wife Back Before It's Too Late: A Game Plan for Reconciling Your Marriage.* Nashville, TN: Thomas Nelson, 1999.

———. *If Only He Knew.* Rev. ed. Grand Rapids, MI: Zondervan Publishing House, 1997.

Top Gun Ministries. *Tackling Men's Toughest Questions* Audiocassette Series. (Order at www.topgunministries.org.)

Women

Berry, Jo. *Beloved Unbeliever: Loving Your Husband into the Faith.* Grand Rapids, MI: Zondervan Publishing House, 1981.

DeMoss, Nancy Leigh, ed. *Biblical Womanhood in the Home.* Wheaton, IL: Crossway Books, 2002.

Eldredge, John. *Wild at Heart: Discovering the Passionate Soul of a Man.* Nashville, TN: Thomas Nelson, 2001.

Leman, Kevin. *Making Sense of the Men in Your Life: What Makes Them Tick, What Ticks You Off and How to Live in Harmony.* Nashville, TN: Thomas Nelson, 2000.

Means, Marsha. *Living with Your Husband's Secret Wars.* Grand Rapids, MI: Fleming H. Revell, 1999.

Morley, Patrick M. *What Husbands Wish Their Wives Knew About Men.* Grand Rapids, MI: Zondervan Publishing House, 1998.

Omartian, Stormie. *The Power of a Praying Wife.* Eugene, OR: Harvest House, 1997.

Peace, Martha. *The Excellent Wife: A Biblical Perspective.* Bemidji, MN: Focus Publishing, Inc., 1995.

Smalley, Gary and Greg. *Winning Your Husband Back Before It's Too Late.* Nashville, TN: Thomas Nelson, 1999.

Smith, Debra White. *Romancing Your Husband.* Eugene, OR: Harvest House, 2002.

Snyder, Chuck. *Men: Some Assembly Required.* Wheaton, IL: Tyndale House Publishers, 1995.

Emotional Healing

Hemfelt, Robert; Frank Minirth; and Paul Meier. *Love Is a Choice: Recovery for Codependent Relationships.* Nashville, TN: Thomas Nelson, 1989.

Sledge, Tim. *Making Peace with Your Past: Help for Adult Children of Dysfunctional Families.* Nashville, TN: LifeWay Press, 1992.

Turning Point Ministries. *Anger: Our Master or Our Servant.* (Order at www.turningpointministries.org.)

——. *Completely Free.* (Order at www.turningpointministries.org.)

——. *Concerned Persons.* (Order at www.turningpointministries.org.)

Wright, H. Norman. *Making Peace with Your Past.* Old Tappan, NJ: Fleming H. Revell, 1985.

Ministry Development and Worker Training

General

Barna, George. *The Power of Team Leadership: Achieving Success Through Shared Responsibility.* Colorado Springs, CO: WaterBrook Press, 2001.

Rinehart, Stacy. *Upside Down: The Paradox of Servant Leadership.* Colorado Springs, CO: NavPress, 1998.

Strengthening Marriages in Your Community: 101 Ideas to Get You Started. Washington, DC: A and E Family Publishers, 2002.

Small Groups

Accountability Groups

Helton, Jeff and Lora. *Authentic Marriage: How to Connect with Other Couples Through a Marriage Accountability Group.* Chicago: Moody Press, 1999.

Home Groups

Comiskey, Joel. *How to Lead a Small Group Meeting So People Want to Come Back.* Houston, TX: Cell Group Resources, 2001.

Donahue, Bill. *The Willow Creek Guide to Leading Life-Changing Small Groups.* Grand Rapids, MI: Zondervan Publishing House, 1996.

Support Groups

Christian Recovery Connection. *Alcoholics Victorious Manual.* (Order at www.alcoholicsvictorious.org.)

O'Neil, Mike S., and Charles E. Newbold, Jr. *The Church as a Healing Community: Setting Up Shop to Deal with the Pain of Life-Controlling Problems.* Nashville, TN: Sonlight Publishing, 1994.

Ketterman, Grace H. *Verbal Abuse.* Ann Arbor, MI: Servant Publications, 1992.

Wilson, Sandra. *Released from Shame: Moving Beyond the Pain of the Past.* Downers Grove, IL: InterVarsity Press, 1990.

Mentoring

Anderson, Keith R., and Randy L. Reese. *Spiritual Mentoring: A Guide for Seeking and Giving Direction.* Downers Grove, IL: InterVarsity Press, 1999.

McManus, Michael J. *Marriage Savers: Helping Your Friends and Family Avoid Divorce.* Grand Rapids, MI: Zondervan Publishing House, 1995.

———. *Manual to Create a Marriage Savers Congregation.* (Order at www.marriagesavers.com.)

National Association of Marriage Enhancement. Lay Couple Counseling Training Series [Video]. (Order at 1-888-262-NAME [1-888-262-6263].)

chapter sixteen

HELPFUL WEBSITES

Here are a few online organizations that provide helpful resources, information and services to strengthen marriages.

General Marriage and Family Information

http://www.citizenlink.org
A site dedicated to providing articles on hot marriage topics and family issues.

http://www.family.org
Focus on the Family's site; provides great links to several diverse marriage and family resources and articles.

Divorce Information

http://www.divorceresourcecenter.com
A great site with articles, links and more to support those in unwanted pending divorce situations.

http://www.preventingdivorce.com
Dedicated to providing resources for divorce prevention, including books, articles and links to other websites.

Help with Addictions

http://www.christianrecovery.com
A coalition of ministries dedicated to helping the Christian community become a safe and helpful place for people recovering from addiction, abuse or trauma.

http://www.sexaddict.com
For addicts and/or their loved ones. Includes "Am I a Sex Addict?" quiz, links to support groups, e-mail forum, resources and more.

http://www.turningpointministries.org
For those struggling to break free from addiction, anger and depression.

Marriage-Building Resources

http://smalley.gospelcom.net
Packed with great resources, conference ideas and upcoming material.

http://marriagedivorce.com
Dedicated to the restoration of Christian marriage. Includes links to other Christian sites for marriage, divorce and remarriage.

http://www.marriagebuilders.com
Features practical articles written by Willard F. Harley, Jr., Ph.D., discussion forum and much more.

http://www.smartmarriages.com
A fantastic site by the Coalition for Marriage, Family, and Couples Education, L.L.C.

http://www.uchicago.edu/divinity/family
A scholarly site dedicated to the plight of contemporary American families.

http://user.aol.com/openbible/450.html
The Bible Research Library site with essays and studies from the Word of God on marriage, divorce and related topics.

http://www.relationships.com
From the Center for Relationship Development, featuring a resource library, great links and Les and Leslie Parrot's speaking schedule.

Programs and Conferences

http://www.istilldo.com
Affiliated with Promise Keepers.

http://www.familylife.com
A division of Campus Crusade for Christ.

http://www.nameonline.net
Homepage of National Association of Marriage Enhancement, a ministry designed to equip churches to become marriage hospitals.

http://www.marriagesavers.org
Designed to help couples prepare for lifelong marriage, strengthen existing marriages and restore troubled marriages.

http://www.marriage.org
Homepage of University of the Family, which ministers to families around the world through in-home courses, seminar tapes and books.

http://folksites.com/repairing-the-breach
Homepage of Repairing the Breach Marriage Ministry, dedicated to the reminder that reconciliation is possible through the power of God.

http://www.covenantkeepersinc.org
Features online newsletters and prayer and information about the Covenant Keepers ministry.

http://www.completemarriages.com
Home of Complete Marriages marriage seminars, featuring an online marriage club, telephone marriage counseling and program resources.

http://www.marriagealive.com
Features Marriage Builders tips, articles, ideas (e.g., *10 Great Dates*) and Marriage Alive University Online (for college credit).

Welcome to the Family!

As you participate in the *Focus on the Family Marriage Series*, it is our prayerful hope that God will deepen your understanding of His plan for marriage and that He will strengthen your marriage relationship.

This series is just one of the many helpful, insightful, and encouraging resources produced by Focus on the Family. In fact, that's what Focus on the Family is all about—providing inspiration, information, and biblically based advice to people in all stages of life.

It began in 1977 with the vision of one man, Dr. James Dobson, a licensed psychologist and author of 18 best-selling books on marriage, parenting, and family. Alarmed by the societal, political, and economic pressures that were threatening the existence of the American family, Dr. Dobson founded Focus on the Family with one employee and a once-a-week radio broadcast aired on only 36 stations.

Now an international organization, the ministry is dedicated to preserving Judeo-Christian values and strengthening and encouraging families through the life-changing message of Jesus Christ. Focus ministries reach families worldwide through 10 separate radio broadcasts, two television news features, 13 publications, 18 Web sites, and a steady series of books and award-winning films and videos for people of all ages and interests.

We'd love to hear from you!

For more information about the ministry, or if we can be of help to your family, simply write to Focus on the Family, Colorado Springs, CO 80995 or call 1-800-A-FAMILY (1-800-232-6459). Friends in Canada may write Focus on the Family, P.O. Box 9800, Stn. Terminal, Vancouver, B.C. V6B 4G3 or call 1-800-661-9800. Visit our Web site—www.family.org—to learn more about Focus on the Family or to find out if there is an associate office in your country.

Strengthen and enrich your marriage with these Focus on the Family® relationship builders.

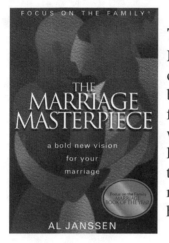

The Marriage Masterpiece

Now that you've discovered the richness to be had in "The Focus on the Family Marriage Series" Bible studies, be sure to read the book the series is based on. *The Marriage Masterpiece* takes a fresh appraisal of the exquisite design God has for a man and woman. Explaining the reasons why this union is meant to last a lifetime, it also shows how God's relationship with humanity is the model for marriage. Rediscover the beauty and worth of marriage in a new light with this thoughtful, creative book. A helpful study guide is included for group discussion. Hardcover.

The Love List

Marriage experts Drs. Les and Leslie Parrot present eight healthy habits that refresh, transform and restore the intimacy of your marriage relationship. Filled with practical suggestions, this book will help you make daily, weekly, monthly and yearly improvements in your marriage. Hardcover.

Capture His Heart/Capture Her Heart

Lysa TerKeurst has written two practical guides—one for wives and one for husbands—that will open your eyes to the needs, desires and longings of your spouse. These two books each offer eight essential criteria plus creative tips for winning and holding his or her heart. Paperback set.

• • •

Look for these special books in your Christian bookstore or request a copy by calling 1-800-A-FAMILY (1-800-232-6459). Friends in Canada may write Focus on the Family, P.O. Box 9800, Stn. Terminal, Vancouver, B.C. V6B 4G3 or call 1-800-661-9800.

Visit our Web site (www.family.org) to learn more about the ministry or find out if there is a Focus on the Family office in your country.